SELLING SCIENCE

How to Use Business Skills to Win Support for Scientific Research

Titles of Interest

Crackle and Fizz: Essential Communication and Pitching Skills for Scientists
by Caroline van den Brul
ISBN: 978-1-78326-283-0
ISBN: 978-1-78326-284-7 (pbk)

Communicating Science: A Practical Guide for Engineers and Physical Scientists
by Raymond Boxman and Edith Boxman
ISBN: 978-981-3144-22-4
ISBN: 978-981-3144-23-1 (pbk)

The Grant Writer's Handbook: How to Write a Research Proposal and Succeed
by Gerard M Crawley and Eoin O'Sullivan
ISBN: 978-1-78326-759-0
ISBN: 978-1-78326-414-8 (pbk)

The Grant Writing and Crowdfunding Guide for Young Investigators in Science
by Jean-Luc Lebrun and Justin Lebrun
ISBN: 978-981-3223-23-3
ISBN: 978-981-3223-24-0 (pbk)

Planning Your Research and How to Write It
edited by Aziz Nather
ISBN: 978-981-4651-03-5
ISBN: 978-981-4651-04-2 (pbk)

SELLING SCIENCE

How to Use Business Skills to Win
Support for Scientific Research

Steven Judge
Richard Lucas

With a foreword by
Professor Paddy Regan

 **World Scientific**

RSEY · LONDON · SINGAPORE · BEIJING · SHANGHAI · HONG KONG · TAIPEI · CHENNAI · TOKYO

Published by

World Scientific Publishing Europe Ltd.

57 Shelton Street, Covent Garden, London WC2H 9HE

Head office: 5 Toh Tuck Link, Singapore 596224

USA office: 27 Warren Street, Suite 401-402, Hackensack, NJ 07601

Library of Congress Cataloging-in-Publication Data
Names: Judge, S. M. (Steven M.), author.
Title: Selling science : how to use business skills to win support for scientific research /
    Steven Judge (National Physical Laboratory, United Kingdom),
    Richard Lucas (National Physical Laboratory, United Kingdom).
Description: New Jersey : World Scientific, [2018] | Includes bibliographical references and index.
Identifiers: LCCN 2018014027 | ISBN 9781786345721 (hc : alk. paper)
Subjects: LCSH: Research, Industrial. | Science and industry. | New products. | Marketing.
Classification: LCC T175 .J83 2018 | DDC 658.8--dc23
LC record available at https://lccn.loc.gov/2018014027

British Library Cataloguing-in-Publication Data
A catalogue record for this book is available from the British Library.

For any available supplementary material, please visit
http://www.worldscientific.com/worldscibooks/10.1142/Q0170#t=suppl

Desk Editors: Anthony Alexander/Jennifer Brough/Koe Shi Ying

Typeset by Stallion Press
Email: enquiries@stallionpress.com

Printed in Singapore

This book is dedicated to the physicists, chemists, biologists, mathematicians and engineers, whose research helps to improve the quality of life for so many people worldwide

Foreword

All scientists rely on the simplistic core concept of funding to get their research underway and continued. The cycle of regular application, failure, rejection, occasional success, re-application, re-failure, occasional re-success is common for the majority of the professional research scientist class. In the contemporary era, while there are arguably greater levels of funding resource than ever before, paradoxically, the competition for these finite resources is fiercer than ever. The funding agencies and industrial sponsors want value for money for their input, be it in terms of ultimate commercial gain, ideally linking this with pushing the 'best science forwards'. The concept of impact of the research is pervasive throughout, with researchers being required to demonstrate both the usefulness, interesting science and ultimate economic value of their research from the nascent emergence until its final fruition. From my own experience, the realised impact is often only clear some years after the end of the research period, but is often not at all clear in the initial launch period or during the research working period. Research scientists are, in general, woefully unprepared for understanding the business and economic aspects, and indeed final impacts of their research work. This can lead to much wasted time where scientists apply for larger and larger grants with smaller and smaller chances of success.

This excellent and unique book by Steven Judge and Richard Lucas aims to lead the working researcher through the myriad of different marketing and business skill sets which scientists are often not even remotely aware of. These allow the research scientist to be much better prepared on the aspects of 'selling the science' at the start of the research journey and embed these aspects into the entire project. Important aspects such as information gathering; analysis of these data; understanding your stakeholder, customers, and competitors; marketing; SWOT analyses; financial and commercial reality checks; pricing; employments aspects and final outputs such as patents vs. published papers are all explained in a clear straightforward fashion. The book also gives a wide range of easy-to-follow examples which demonstrate the use of these tools across all scientific research sectors, including what might have in the past been described as 'blue skies, curiosity driven' research. Judge and Lucas bring decades of real-world experience to this work, including initial research background in fundamental nuclear physics, broader 'industrial' research and provision, marketing, business strategy and management of some of the largest radiological standards bodies in the world.

This is an outstandingly well written and very useful tool for all ranges of scientific researchers in the preparation of their future grant and research proposals. It shines a light in an area where most professional day-to-day scientists have been traditionally ill-prepared, but gives them information which they need to be armed with into the 21st century, I would certainly recommend this as a 'must-read' primer for those starting out on their independent researcher journey and also for more experienced research scientists who are trying to get to grips with the continually changing nature of securing research funding.

Paddy Regan
National Physical Laboratory
Professor of Radionuclide Metrology

19 December 2017

Preface

This book came into being through wanting to help all those scientists carrying out the scientific research that has so much impact on the world, but is often not appreciated. With some frustration at this situation, we turned to the work of professional marketers to look for ideas on how to win funding for research and to sell the ideas and products that result. What we found was that you have to plan for your work to have impact — over the years, we have tried to put this into practice, and this book is based on our experience.

Particular thanks are due to Professor Malcolm McDonald, a leading marketing expert and inspirational speaker. The encouragement of Dr Brian Bowsher, Chief Executive of the UK Science and Technology Facilities Council, is gratefully acknowledged. The authors are also extremely grateful to Mr Samuel Judge, Chartered Patent Attorney, for his comments on the section on intellectual property law.

The authors wish to thank all of their colleagues who contributed one way or another to this work — Dr Mike Goldsmith (physicist and author), Dr Martyn Sené (Deputy Director, National Physical Laboratory, UK) and Herr Uwe Beinlich & Herr Olaf Scheibe (ex-Amersham International plc) should be mentioned. Regretfully, there is not enough space to thank everyone, but you know who you are.

Steven Judge and Richard Lucas

About the Authors

Dr Steven Judge was a nuclear physicist at the UK's National Physical Laboratory and the Laue-Langevin Institute in France, before following a career in technical management that included several years as a marketing manager at Amersham International plc (now part of GE Healthcare). He has led successful teams at the National Physical Laboratory, bidding for and delivering multinational projects, working at the interface between academia and industry.

He has a degree in Physics from the University of Oxford, a PhD in radiation physics and post-graduate qualifications in marketing and programme management. He is a Fellow of the Institute of Physics and Director of the Ionizing Radiation Department at the Bureau International des Poids et Mesures, the world focus for the international measurement system.

 **Richard Lucas** has extensive commercial and management experience having worked for Hewlett Packard in Europe for over 20 years. As a certified project and programme manager, he led diverse teams to define and successfully sell major projects to UK government agencies and multinational companies.

Over a subsequent five-year period at the National Physical Laboratory, Richard held a variety of Group Leader positions working across a range of research areas and science disciplines. In this internationally competitive environment, he has provided support and mentoring to research teams seeking funding.

Contents

Chapter 1

Introduction

"Scientific knowledge and technological developments offer unprecedented opportunities for rapid social progress."

Trieste Forum: Impact of Science and Technology on Society and Economy, World Academy of Art & Science, Trieste, 2013

Science offers a fascinating career, whether it is working in research in a university or a national or international laboratory, or contributing to the field in the many commercial companies developing innovative new products and services that benefit society.

Wherever you work and whatever your field, you will no doubt be called on from time to time to make a case for your work, to sell your science, perhaps in a grant application or for work for a customer. You may also be asked to create the new science, the new product or the new service that takes the field forward. You probably have more than enough to do in your day job, and putting together the information you need and working out the next steps can seem to be a distraction.

All too often, scientific research is justified by looking backwards to try to work out what the impact was; this is not a luxury that many organizations can enjoy, nor does it really help win support for the next research programme. The thesis of the authors' work and of this book is that it is much better to plan in advance what the work will achieve, how it will benefit others and how the results will be communicated and used (for the public good or as products that your organization sells). Planning for

1

impact requires ingenuity and inspiration; it often brings new ideas, and is interesting and challenging. It improves the chances of your research making a real difference.

The approach is based on tools from professional marketing, adapted through practical experience for scientific research and development. This book aims to help you gather the information you need and then to analyze it quickly, easily and effectively. It describes a logical sequence of steps, working from the big picture to specific actions, which will ensure that you cover all you need. The first part is concerned with information gathering, next we will use some marketing tools to analyze the data and following that we work out what we will actually do:

It is all about trying to match what your organization does to what your customers want, and communicating with the customers. The tools can, and should, be adapted to your particular organization, but they give a tried-and-tested framework to use.

The last part of the book is some advice, from experience, on how to use the material in the workplace. But really, the book has one simple aim: to pass on what the authors wish they had known earlier in their careers.

Chapter 2

Information Gathering

"Success is a science. If you have the conditions, you will get the result."

Oscar Wilde

In this chapter:

- How to research your market

- How to identify your stakeholders, customers and competitors

2.1 Why Is All This Information Needed?

"But it is obvious why this work is so important!" This is how most discussions about the need for scientific research and development begin. It may well be obvious to people working in the field, but it may not be so clear to funding councils, to politicians, to the general public, to senior management or even to colleagues. Perhaps, it is reasonable sometimes for other people to challenge the value of the work (after all, in some cases, they are paying for it).

The response in academic research is often to try to explain how the work will contribute to solving the problems of society — the 'grand challenges' of ensuring effective healthcare, energy supply, the new digital economy and ensuring a safe and secure environment. Claiming that research into the measurement of, say, a neutron interaction cross-section, underpins the whole of the nuclear energy industry is a long stretch. Of course, it will make a contribution to the industry, but to be something you can use to help sell your work the link needs to be much clearer.

This section helps you gather the information you will need to make your case more specific. There is another benefit as you will need exactly the same information to write the introduction to scientific papers. The three main questions it will help you answer are:

- What are the specific drivers for the work?
- Why should we (rather than another organization) do the work?
- Who will benefit from it?

To make this very useful for you, there is one strict rule to follow. You need objective evidence for all the information — this could be reports, papers, feedback from customer visits, sales data — otherwise it is just your opinion and this may, or may not, be right.

2.2 The Marketing Environment

The first step is to gather the information on the external factors that have an impact on your organization, in the short and long term. Big picture issues such as changes in society, changes in regulations and changes in

Your
environment

Your market

Your
organization

**The marketing
environment**
Your organization exists
in an environment
(regulations, technology,
economy, society) and is
affected by your
immediate market of
customers, competitors
and suppliers.

technology may affect your organization in the future much more than may come to mind. Your competitors and customers may have shorter term effects on your organization. All of these factors, in marketing jargon, are called the marketing environment.

So the first step is to gather the information on your marketing environment, starting with the long-term trends.

2.3 Gathering Information on the Long-Term Trends

"The Americans have need of the telephone, but we do not. We have plenty of messenger boys."

Sir William Preece, Chief Engineer, Royal Mail, UK, 1878

Science is a long-term game. It can take many years before a new instrument or method is adopted — after all — as Sir William Preece said in the quote above, why should any organization invest in something new and expensive unless there is a strong motivation?

The essential first step in analyzing the market is to find out the big picture, the long-term trends that could influence your customers and your organization. This is useful from a business perspective but also from a scientific point of view; any research you do on this will help you write the introductions to scientific papers or presentations. In marketing, this is called PEST analysis, where you structure the analysis to take into account Political, Economic, Social and Technological factors.

To make PEST analysis more useful in a scientific market, it can help to be more specific by first identifying all groups that could have an influence on or an interest in the field (the stakeholders). Stakeholders typically include:

- Regulatory bodies (such as Health & Safety organizations, environmental protection agencies, pharmaceutical licensing authorities).
- Professional bodies (for example, the Institute of Physics, Royal Society of Chemistry, international societies).
- Government departments.
- Research Funding Councils (such as the Science and Technology Facilities Council in the UK).

- Funding bodies and charitable funding bodies (Innovate UK, Wellcome Trust…).
- Universities.
- International organizations (the World Health Organization, WHO; the International Atomic Energy Agency, IAEA; etc.).
- National and international committees.
- Standards bodies (for example, International Organization for Standardization (ISO)) and national accreditation bodies (organizations that are affiliated to ILAC (the international organization for accreditation bodies), such as UKAS, DAkkS, CoFRAC).

It may also be worth considering direct customers and competitors as stakeholders as well, although we will gather more detailed information on both these groups in more detail in the next sections.

A quick graphical representation (a stakeholder map) can be useful to get an overview of the main organizations or groups that affect your organization:

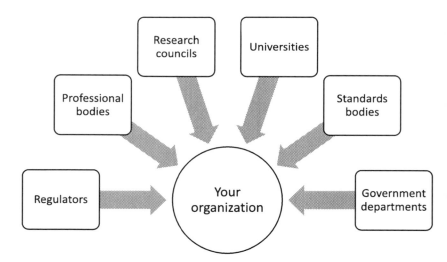

The trick is to list the specific stakeholders that have an effect on your organization — for example, which particular national committee is responsible for defining the Codes of Practice that your customers will be following in the future? Which government department is responsible for policy in your field? Given this list, the next step is to study how they could influence your market in the long term when considering the following questions:

- What are the changes in science and technology that could change your field?
- What are the economic changes (how will funding change)?
- What are the likely changes in laws, regulations, standards or professional good practice guides?
- Are there any changes in society or politics that could be important?

There are many different sources of information you can consult. For changes in science and technology, scientific conferences are a useful source of information, but take the time to visit the industrial exhibition as well as listening to the presentations. Publications by the stakeholders, such as review articles and trade journals will also give you some insights. International organizations, national organizations and professional bodies often publish very thorough reviews. We can't emphasize enough how important it is to look into this topic in detail. Your new product could be wiped out overnight by a new technology developed by a competitor — we've seen it happen, and perhaps if the company had kept an ear to the ground it could have avoided a wasted investment. For any publication you consult, it's worth writing a very brief summary of the contents (a few bullet points) so you can refer back later.

The economic factors that influence your organization can include changes in government spending priorities, but also 'big picture' issues such as currency exchange rates. The importance of regulatory changes are frequently underestimated in science, but often it is only this that will force some organizations to change what they are doing and therefore give you an opportunity to sell your new product or encourage the uptake of your research. The scientists and engineers you talk to may be very clear on the benefits of what you are offering, but within their own organizations they have to fight the case for any changes or costs. It's therefore important to track very carefully what is happening in your sector, including:

- Regulatory changes.
- Changes to international standards (ISO, IEC, etc.).

- Changes to international guidance (for example, standards published by organizations such as the IAEA).
- Changes to national guidance — good practice guides published by professional bodies or national laboratories.

Most scientific products and services are sold business-to-business, so it is easy to write-off changes in society as having no impact on your organization. However, government priorities give a good indication of general issues (for example, ageing population, carbon emissions, encouraging investment in technical training) and are published on the web, discussed in government speeches...

Having reviewed the information available, before moving on to the next stage, it's useful to write a very short summary of your findings and to capture the main points in a table (with references to where the information you are using came from) such as:

Category	Issue	Implications	Evidence
Regulatory	Change in environmental protection regulations	Demand for more accurate measurement of pollutants	New EU Directive
Economic	Reduced government spending	Reduced market for our products	Published budgets
Social	Ageing workforce, high retirement rate	Need for new training initiatives	Review published by professional body
Technology	Need for *in situ* measurement techniques	Move away from traditional lab-based instruments	Report by trade body

Outputs from this stage

- Stakeholder map
- Table summarizing the influences on your organization
- References to where you got the information from
- A very brief summary of the contents of each reference
- A paragraph or two summarizing the big picture issues

2.4 Gathering Information on Customers: Segmentation

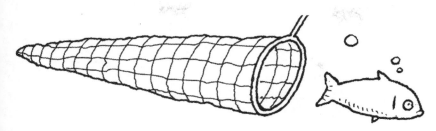

We will use the word 'customer' to mean the organizations or individuals that use the outcomes from your work, and 'selling' to mean the process of persuading them to use what you do. Depending on what your organization is aiming to do, they may be customers in the usual sense of the word (i.e. they pay your organization for a product or service), but your organization may be, for example, government funded and you want to ensure that society makes best use of what you do. Whether money changes hands or not, 'customer' is a reasonable word to use as they are consuming what you do in some way, and your organization 'sells' what it does to them.

However you interpret the 'customers' of your organization, it is a truism that 'people buy from people'. This is a challenge for organizations selling their products or services — you need to build a relationship with individual customers, but this can take enormous time and effort (and you need some people back in the laboratory to do the actual work). On the other hand, treating the customers equally won't work either, as you want your communication and products to match what they are interested in.

The trick is to divide the customers up into manageable groups. Each group should be large enough to be worthwhile to think about, but each group should have something about them that makes them different (it could be the products they buy, where they are based, the type of work they do, or the benefits they seek from their purchases). You can then visit a few people in the group, find out what they are interested in and target each group with the relevant products or services. Much cheaper to do than visiting everyone in your database and more interesting to do than sitting in the traffic jams on the motorway network to visit them.

There are other benefits from going through a process to divide customers into groups. You can perhaps identify the customers that are missing from your database, which could help you grow sales or identify where there is an unmet need. You can also have a rough guess at the total market size for your products or services. Within an organization, this is probably the most important piece of information you will need — setting completely unrealistic sales targets seem to be a condition of managing organizations these days, and knowing the total market size with data to back it up will help you escape the clutches of some senior management.

In marketing jargon, dividing up and conquering your customer base in this way is called segmentation and it is at the core of professional marketing. This chapter shows an approach you could use to do this — the key point is not to rush in immediately and choose what may seem to be the obvious segments, but to gather some information first.

Step 1: Plan the approach

At this point in developing a marketing plan, most marketing textbooks recommend investing in qualitative and quantitative market research. In the scientific world, the markets are usually relatively small and the cost of such exercises can exceed any benefit. On the other hand, you have the advantage that it is easy to empathize with your customers who often face the same day-to-day issues you do, and you can take advantage of this.

It's useful to have some structure for a discussion with customers. You should already know who buys which product, so the first part is to get together with colleagues and try to identify what benefits your customers are seeking — from their perspective, what do they want. These could include:

- Saving cost (lower capital cost, lower running costs)
- Saving time
- Meeting a regulation, national or international standard or good practice guide
- A specialist skill to help them develop a new product or service
- Fast turnaround on orders
- After-sales service

- Instrumentation or techniques with better accuracy, better sensitivity, better range, more robust, smaller, portable
- To enable your customer to introduce innovative solutions in their workplace, to develop their own career

From these initial discussions, agree on some questions you could ask your customer to find out in more detail what they really want. You may be surprised by their answers.

Step 2: Identifying what the customers really want

In this step, it is important to keep at the back of your mind that you are looking for what the customer wants, not necessarily what you think they need. You may be able to persuade the customer that you are right in the end — but probably not yet.

You can't beat visiting a customer in their place of work to find out what they want. It is very helpful to take with you a list of questions to ask and to take notes — this may seem awkward at first and your first few discussions may be stilted, but this is all about practice and very quickly you won't need to take the list with you (nor will you need to take notes — just write down the main points soon after the meeting).

In formulating the questions, no doubt you have been told in various courses about the difference between 'closed' and 'open' questions (a closed question can be answered with a single word or a short phrase, an open question requires a longer answer and usually starts with 'How, why, what'). Closed questions are easy to answer, and can be very useful in helping the person you are talking to feel at ease, or to check facts and understanding. Open questions are asking for more interpretation. There's a variation of open questions that authors have found to be very useful called 'high gain questions'. This type of question asks the person to think very carefully about the answer through asking them to make some sort of judgement, "How would you compare xxx to yyyy?", "If we could do one thing to help your organization, what would it be?". The key here is that people need time to think about their answer — give them time, wait in silence for the answer! And be sparing with these questions, otherwise any discussions become too intense.

It may not always be possible to meet your customers face-to-face, but there are other approaches you can try. Scientific conferences, industrial exhibitions, professional training events, workshops are all good opportunities to build a network of contacts in the field and to discuss issues that customers face. Any customer complaints recorded in the quality system are excellent indicators of what is really important to them — any positive feedback you've received is also very helpful. You may find you have a colleague who has worked for a customer — they are an excellent source of information (it is a strange quirk of human nature that most organizations don't want to listen to colleagues — try to keep an open mind and guard against this tendency).

Other methods include mailing or emailing out questionnaires to customers. These tend to have very low response rates, even if there is some incentive to respond.

Step 3: List possible segments

Armed with the information from the customers and the background information on long-term trends, you are now in a good position to identify the main segments. There are lots of ways to group the customers together:

- By product range
- By end customer (if your customers work in turn for other customers)
- By location
- By size or type of customer's organization (small/medium enterprise, multinational company, government body, international organization, etc.)

In science though, there is another very useful way to segment the customers, particularly if you are not trying to sell a product but to convince people that your work is valued and is needed: segment the customers by their different roles within the organization. You may well find that the people are looking for different benefits from what you are offering: the technicians may be looking for something that makes their working lives easier, researchers may be looking for novel approaches that can contribute to the next research paper or their promotion, the Quality Manager may want something to enable the organization demonstrate compliance with a regulation or a quality standard, senior management may be looking for something that saves their organization money or helps their organization in following their long-term strategy. In a nutshell, it can be better to segment customers by grouping them by benefit sought rather than more obvious criteria.

There is no correct answer when defining the segments! Experiment till you find an approach that makes sense for your market. In practice, aim to identify a few segments (by combining smaller segments if needed) — any more than this, and developing effective communication with the segments becomes very difficult.

Step 4: Research the size of each segment

The next step is to estimate the size of each segment — number of customers (existing or potential), sales volume, total market size, trends in the segment (is the number of customers in this segment likely to increase or decrease?). Historical sales records, web searches, competitor sales records (from their annual reports, for example), numbers of attendees at conferences, trade shows are all good sources of information.

Here is also where your scientific expertise comes into play. For each segment, you will have a pretty shrewd idea of what a typical customer will need and can have a good estimate at how much a customer will spend with your organization or your competitors every year. Multiply that up by the number of customers in the segment and you will have a pretty good estimate of the total market size.

Step 5: Summarize the information

Finally, pull all the information together into a simple table with the key points. If the aim is to sell a product, it might be something like:

Segment	Who are they?	What do they need?	How much do they spend?	Expanding?
Analytical Laboratories	35 laboratories, within large consultancy companies such as ...	Reference materials	Approximately £25k/year each, total	No — companies making efficiency savings

Once you've populated the table, stand back from what you have done, look at it critically[a] and ask yourself:

- What is missing?
- Do I have evidence to back up each of the entries, however imprecise?

Next try to fill these gaps wherever possible. One of the challenges in the scientific field, and hence a potential gap, is to identify the needs of the users of your work, as much of your work may result in intangible benefits. It can be very useful to draw up a 'benefit map'[b] which shows in stages how the outputs from your work lead to benefits for the ultimate users. A simple example of a benefit map (for products/services for the nuclear industry) is shown below:

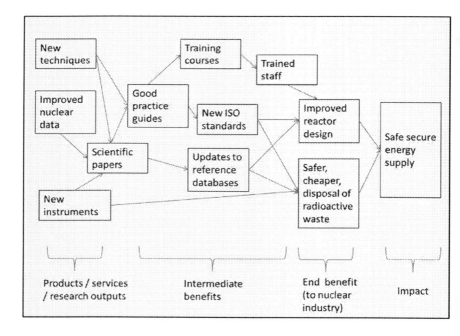

---

[a]The psychologist Edward de Bono refers to this as 'putting on a black hat' in his book *Six Thinking Hats*.
[b]Managing Successful Programmes, Office of Government Commerce, TSO 2007.

The benefit map is useful to work back from what the customers need to what your organization can provide, particularly if your organization's principal aim is to create an impact on society rather than sales revenue.

The table below lists typical intermediate and end benefits as a checklist for developing the benefit map:

Products/services/research outputs	Intermediate benefits	End benefits
New techniques for measurement, production New instruments Intellectual property New knowledge of fundamental Physics/Chemistry/Biology, etc. Scientific papers Conference presentations Newsletters Websites Laboratory consumables/kits Software	Training Documentary standards (national/international) and technical specifications Improved information in databases Intellectual property for exploitation through licences	Cost savings Higher accuracy Competitive advantage Regulatory compliance

The benefit map will also be very useful when it comes to measuring the effectiveness of the plans you will develop.

So you now have a good idea of long-term trends in your market and what your customers want. You can also identify which of your customer segments are important — perhaps an area that is growing rapidly will be more important than a large segment that is declining?

The next challenge is that your competitors are also trying to meet the demand from the customers. It's best to find out about the competitors as well, and that is the topic of the next section.

Outputs from this stage

- A table showing the customer segments you have chosen
- A summary of what each customer segment wants (or perhaps needs)
- Notes on where you got the information from
- A paragraph or two summarizing the customer segments

2.5 Competitor Analysis: Know Your Enemy

The authors still find astonishing the number of meetings they have endured during which they have been challenged about why the organization is not doing £10 million of business in a particular market, or why the organization is not recognized as leading the impact in the field. Of course, the reason is that we are not the only organization to have recognized opportunities in a particular field — the competitors have got there first.

Even if your organization does not sell products as such but is working on research for the public good, it is still worthwhile spending time analyzing what other organizations are doing in the field, to help you decide where your work can have the most impact. It may not be worth competing directly with a large, experienced, research group working in exactly the same field. Or you may be competing with them to get there first in the race to the new discovery so you will need to know what progress they are making.

As first pointed out by Michael Porter of Harvard University,[c] your organization may face more competitors than first meet the eye.

---

[c] Michael E. Porter, "How Competitive Forces Shape Strategy," *Harvard Business Review*, May 1979 (Vol. 59, No. 2), pp. 137–145.

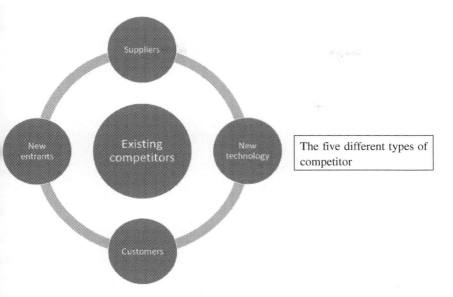

The five different types of competitor

(1) **Existing competitors supplying products or services that compete with you**
These are the people you already see at industrial exhibitions or meet at scientific conferences, workshops, committees, etc. For scientific R&D, universities are probably major competitors. You probably know most of this type of competitor or a web search will identify most of them easily.

(2) **Organizations to which you supply your products**
You could face new competition from organizations that you supply at the moment — your customers or your stakeholders. There is an irony that if an organization finds your work very valuable, it may set up its own capability that will compete with you.

(3) **Suppliers to your organization**
Your suppliers are also worth reviewing, as they also understand your business: they probably know the market well, know your customers and the products/services they want, and perhaps they are in a good position to compete with you directly. Suppliers will be more powerful if there are few of them and few substitutes.

(4) **New products**
Worst of all for any organization working in science and technology, probably the most difficult to identify is someone with a bright idea

which gets rid of the need for your services completely. The digital camera to your film camera.

(5) **New competitors**
The fifth type of competitor that Porter identified is the new player, organizations, for example, from overseas whom you've not come across before, or organizations working in similar markets (for example, the nuclear industry is turning to suppliers in other heavily-regulated sectors).

By now, you will probably have in your mind a list of many different organizations that could compete. But don't despair! In practice, there may be factors that can dissuade competitors from entering the market; these 'barriers to entry' are worth thinking about as well, to get a feeling for how likely it is for a new competitor to enter the market. Some of the possible barriers to entry are listed in the table below; organizations can also be dissuaded from investing if there could be barriers to exiting a market if the investment doesn't work out: for example, potential difficulties in selling specialist equipment and legal and moral obligations to staff.

Regulatory	Compliance with health and safety regulations Site licenses that are needed to carry out work with hazardous materials Routes for the disposal of any hazardous wastes
Financial	Investment needed in building infrastructure, instrumentation and software Cost of licenses for use of any patents owned by other organizations Investment in safety equipment
Skills	Recruitment of skilled staff Staff training
Systems	Investment in developing procedures and in validating techniques Accreditation to international standards New software systems
Marketing	Access to customers Costs of setting up a website, attending industrial exhibitions

2.5.1 *Gathering Information on Competitors*

So it is very important to find out who your existing and potential competitors are, and to gather some key information on them — information that will help you plan how to promote your products and services, or even assess whether it is worthwhile remaining in the market. You also get some ideas on what you could be doing or early warnings of threats and opportunities. In fact, it is so important to the organizations that some have resorted to the dubious practice of going through their competitor's bins for information[d]!

Gathering information about competitors is best done as a group exercise. It helps to share information of course, but a hidden benefit is that seeing how much better your competitors are doesn't half wake up reluctant members of the group. The sudden realization that the competitor's website is much better turns updating the website from a chore at the bottom of the pile to something that must be done urgently.

There is a lot of potential information that you could assemble. In a scientific market, the key information you need is detailed in the following paragraphs.

2.5.1.1 Who They Are

It is usually fairly easy to identify your existing competitors from:

- Web searches
- Attendances at industrial exhibitions and scientific conferences
- Articles and advertisements in trade journals
- Attendance at meetings where funding organizations are explaining invitations to tender

Looking at which organizations are recruiting in your field can also be an indication.

Identifying possible new competitors is more difficult, but it is worth discussing whether your suppliers or customers may be considering setting up to do the work (this does happen in the authors' experience, and

---

[d] See the examples in Gary Armstrong *et al.*, *Marketing: An Introduction*. Pearson Education Ltd., London, 2009.

perhaps if they had been alert to the possibility at the time a new competitor could have been avoided by offering a better/cheaper service).

2.5.1.2 What They Sell into the Market You Are Interested in

The web is of course the major source of detailed information on your competitor's existing products. Finding out what they are planning can be more difficult, but patent applications can give you some clues (as listed on, for example, the European Patent Office website www.epo.org).

2.5.1.3 What Market Share They Have

This is more difficult to find out, but can be very useful. Company annual reports can usually be found on the web and are a great source of information (they may wish to attract investment so are happy to advertise how much work they are doing). Chatting to people from other organizations and putting the information together can also give you some information on this.

2.5.1.4 How They Promote Their Products

This is where you learn some salutary lessons about your own marketing efforts. If you were a customer, how easy is it to find out about the products/services the competitor offers? Do they use local distributors? Write articles in trade journals? Do they have an active sales force? Do they attend industrial exhibitions? What features does their website have — anything better than your own?

2.5.1.5 What Prices Do They Charge

If you have the nerve (and it does take some nerve!), the easiest and most accurate way to find out what your competitors charge is to ask their customers. We've even had one customer who said 'hang on a minute, I'll dig out their most recent invoice'.

You might be able to find out on the web, or colleagues in another part of your organization may use their products. For large contracts it is useful to keep a record of contracts won and lost — some organizations will give feedback on reasons for rejecting your tender and if price is mentioned frequently you can get a pretty good idea of what your competitors charge for their work.

2.5.1.6 How Might They React to Competition?

Finally, it's also worth recording how you think competitors will respond to anything your organization might do. Most organizations will monitor how they are doing, looking for trends, so if your organization is taking sales away or starting new research in 'their' field of work it will be spotted! This can only be based on judgement, but there may be some evidence from past events.

Some competitors will be laid back and not react (perhaps because they have other issues to worry about), they can be selective (they notice what is happening but will react only if it is impacting one of their priorities), they can be tigers (responding immediately to compete, reducing prices or increasing their marketing efforts) or stochastic (unpredictable).

It will only be a guess of course, but how the competitors may react can impact what your organization chooses to do going ahead.

It's useful to summarize what you find out in a table:

Competitor	What do they do that competes with us?	What market share do they have?	What prices do they charge?	How do they promote their products?
Company X	Directly competing range of reference materials	From their annual report, 60%	Approximately 10% lower than ours	Web-based catalogue, sales force, exhibitions

If your organization is focused on research in the public interest, this table would look different but could include factors such as income from research grants, expertise that competes, etc.

Outputs from this stage

- A list of competitors
- A table summarizing how they compete
- Notes on where you got the information from
- A paragraph or two summarizing the competitors

Chapter 3

Analysis

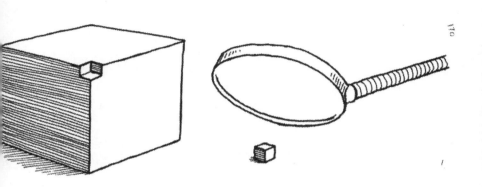

In this chapter:

- How to work out what your organization is good at

- How to find the best market for your work

- What you should include in your long-term strategy

3.1 Introduction

In this part, we will look at three different tools used in marketing to analyze the market. These analysis methods are most useful if used by small groups — the conversation itself is probably more important than any report on the analysis you may write as at the end you should all have a good understanding of how the market works and what your organization should do.

Many different analysis tools have been developed by different organizations over the years, with many different variations. Here are three of these tools that are easy to use, often lead to unexpected insights and lead in a logical way to a strategy that shows where your organization might invest its efforts.

The sequence is:

(a) Work out your advantages (using strengths, weaknesses, opportunities, and threats (SWOT) analysis).
(b) Work out which parts of the market play to your strengths (market attractiveness analysis).
(c) Work out your strategy, taking account of the risks (create an Ansoff matrix).

The first of these tools (SWOT analysis) originated from work at Stanford University in the USA in the 1960s and 1970s, the aim of the work being to identify why corporate planning failed. The research identified key areas that affected an organization, and it resulted in a simple tool that is still used today by many organizations to work out what is important to them. SWOT analysis can be very useful to identify what your organization needs to do to improve, and to recognize general opportunities which the organization can exploit (for financial gain or for the impact from the work).

The authors have participated in SWOT analysis sessions in commercial companies and in large research institutes, and found it can give some insights to guide what the organization should do. However, its very popularity as a technique means that it sometimes gets the reaction 'oh no, not again' from participants and it is all too easy to end up with the same conclusions that all organizations working in the field would have. The SWOT analysis described in the next section avoids this by looking at the tool from another point of view and making it semi-quantitative.

Another disadvantage of SWOT analysis is that it is difficult to use it to review the products and services that your organization offers in detail. The next tool, the market attractiveness matrix, helps you reflect on products, or groups of products, or different customer segments and pick out which products/services should be invested in. Its origins lie in the well-known (amongst marketers) work of the Boston Consulting Group (BGC) in 1968. BGC considered that there were two factors that were important in deciding where to invest: the potential growth in the market for the products/services and the organization's share of that market. The BGC analysis puts the products/services into four categories:

- 'Stars' — fast growing market, high share of the market — to be invested in, but can cost more than the revenue brought in.
- 'Cash cows' — slow growing market, high market share. These products tend to generate more cash than they consume and should be used to support other products.
- 'Question marks' — fast growing market but low market share at present. Building the market share can be costly and risky, but the products could turn into stars.
- 'Dogs' — slow growing market, low market share, generating little profit for the organization. These products are prime candidates to be closed down or sold off to another organization.

The disadvantage of the BGC approach is that it only considers two factors (market share and market growth) and assumes the aim of the organization is to maximize profit. The market attractiveness matrix followed on from BGC and was developed by GE and McKinsey in the 1970s to take account of more factors. The approach described in this book is a variant of the GE/McKinsey work, to take into account that much scientific endeavour can be a 'public good' rather than aiming solely to generate profit for the organization. That said, 'public goods' are generally funded from taxation and so the market attractiveness matrix can help you identify where the money can be spent for the maximum impact.

The third tool that we will describe is the Ansoff strategy matrix. It is named after a Russian–American applied mathematician called Igor Ansoff who first published the concept in 1957. It is recommended here as a tool that is used to drag discussions back to reality! In the authors' experience, the temptation is always to concentrate on the new, exciting, challenging ideas and the existing work that is very important can be forgotten. The Ansoff strategy matrix is a salutary reminder that new ideas are very interesting, but they can also be very risky, and so any organization should aim to balance investment in new ideas with maintaining some of the old ones.

The three tools described aim to enable a measured, objective, rational discussion of what your organization does and what it could do. Everyone present in the discussions will have an opinion on what your organization should be doing, and it is all too easy to jump to conclusions. The tools aim to take the emotion out of the discussions, to structure the analysis carefully and to give the 'slow' part of the brain a chance to work.[a]

3.2 SWOT Analysis

SWOT analysis looks both at factors that are under our control (strengths and weaknesses) and factors that are not under our control (opportunities and threats).

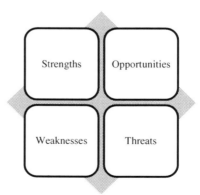

---

[a] Daniel Kahneman, *Thinking Fast and Slow*, Penguin Group (2011).

To make the most of this tool, it can be useful to use it in a semi-quantitative way rather than just list the issues. We'd bet if you visit any laboratory and discuss SWOT analysis, you will end up with a list of weaknesses that includes 'obsolete equipment', 'changes to software very slow to implement', 'not enough storage space for laboratory consumables' and so on. SWOT analysis is partly about factors that can be changed to influence how well the organization does in the market, not an excuse to grumble! Grumbling is what the management meeting is for.

Here is a way that you can use the 'strengths and weaknesses' part of this tool that does not just result in a list of the usual complaints. First, list the critical success factors — what must the organization do right to meet what the customers want? For example, do the customers want fast turnaround, low prices, high accuracy, accreditation to a particular standard? A checklist of issues to take into account is shown below:

Cost	Convenience	Product
— Price of items/service	— Local contact	— Customized
— Price of consumables	— Fast delivery	— Reliable
— Price of service contract	— Repair service	— Ease of use
	— Technical support	
	— Technical knowledge of customer requirements	
Compliance	**Benefits**	**Intangible benefits**
— Regulations	— Improved accuracy	— Strong brand
— Best practice	— Faster in use	— Recognized expertise

List the top few factors and then score them out of 100 (the total should add up to 100). Of course, this is very rough and ready, but the discussion can be very interesting, particularly if you have someone in the group who used to work for one of your customers. (There is a tendency to overrule the people who have relevant experience in favour of the corporate pet assumptions. This is frustrating for both sides — if the individual goes quiet, they are probably thinking 'you idiot, you don't have a clue' but are too polite to say so. Guard against this, your organization could be missing a trick.)

Anyway, record the critical success factors and the scores in a table like the one below:

Critical success factor	Importance to customer	Score	Justification
Price	◄ ▌ ▶	16	Feedback from customer visits
Rapid delivery	◄ ▌ ▶	10	Complaints have been recorded
Technical support line	◄ ▐ ▶	21	Very positive feedback
Speed of repair service	◄ ▌ ▶	27	Feedback from customer visits
Complete product range	◄ ▌ ▶	26	Compatible software, easy-to-use

Now score how well (honestly!) your organization does — you could use a scoring system such as:

0 = we are utterly hopeless,
0.25 = we usually get it wrong,
0.5 = we are mediocre,
0.75 = we have some glitches but we are usually OK,
1.0 = we are very good at this.

Repeat this scoring for your competitors and construct a table that looks like this:

Critical success factors	Your organization	Competitor 1	Competitor 2	Competitor 3
Price	0.25	0.50	0.75	1.00
Rapid delivery	0.50	0.75	0.25	0.25
Technical support line	0.25	0.90	0.80	0.10
Speed of repair service	0.80	0.20	0.40	0.10
Complete product range	0.10	0.90	0.50	0.50

Multiply how important the critical success factors are to the customers by the table showing how well your organization and your competitors do, and you end up with a matrix that looks like:

	Your organization	Competitor 1	Competitor 2	Competitor 3
Price	2	4	5	7
Rapid delivery	6	9	3	3
Technical support line	6	20	18	2
Speed of repair service	26	6	13	3
Complete product range	3	24	13	13

Now you have a semi-quantitative way to review your organization's strengths and weaknesses, and start to analyze what your organization should concentrate on. In the example above, you might conclude:

(a) The rapid repair service seems to be valued by your customers, and it is one of your strengths. Something perhaps to promote more? Or you could perhaps charge more for this? Particularly as price does not seem to be a strong issue.

(b) Your organization is not doing well relative to Competitor 1 as you don't offer a full product range. Perhaps the action is to develop new products?

This approach therefore assesses your organization's strengths and weaknesses, factors that are under your control and helps you pick out what you could do.

The second part of SWOT analysis is to identify the external opportunities and threats. For this, review the information gathered in Chapter 2 and ask yourselves:

- Which parts of the market are expanding?
- Are there new technologies or methods which your organization could adopt?
- Are there new initiatives from the government that will provide opportunities?
- Are new competitors entering the market?

You may need to split this analysis by customer segment or by product, depending on how complex your market is.

Although your organization cannot influence the opportunities and threats, the analysis can help to identify new products you should be offering, so it is worth going through this analysis and recording what you think as part of your action plan (discussed later).

The final part of the analysis is to go back through your conclusions and check if they are self-consistent. For example, the 'strength and weaknesses' analysis may have highlighted that you have an excellent customer helpline, but the 'opportunities and threats' analysis shows that much of the new business is overseas where the helpline has little use.

Outputs from this stage

- A list of what is important to your customers with some justification
- An assessment of how well your organization meets this with justification
- A tentative list of things that your organization needs to do to address any weaknesses or build on strengths
- A list of opportunities and threats
- A paragraph or two summarizing the analysis

3.3 Market Attractiveness

This tool brings together some of the outputs from the SWOT analysis and the market analysis to identify which products or segments your organization should concentrate on, and which areas of work should be dropped.

The first step is to assess the market attractiveness factor. Market attractiveness is the potential of a market (broken down by customer segment or by a group of products, whichever is most useful) to yield returns — whether these returns are financial (sales volume, profitability) or due to other forms of impact (benefits to society). This is a multi-dimensional assessment, taking into account many factors — the competition in the market, the market size, the potential for growth, etc. A checklist is shown below for possible factors to take into account — it depends on your organization what weight you assign to the different factors.

Factors that can make a market more attractive	Factors than can make a market less attractive
Large accessible market (£k)	Small market
Growing market	Declining market
Few competitors	Many competitors
Barriers to new competitors	Easy to enter the market
Few alternative technologies	Many alternative technologies
Many people or organizations impacted by the work	Few people or organizations impacted by the work
Very significant impact on people or organizations (e.g. healthcare)	Long-term trends show declining interest
Long-term potential	Low priority for government
Government priority	

The first step in using this tool is to score the market attractiveness out of 100. A score of 100 might, for example, correspond to a large, growing market with barriers that prevent competitors entering the market. If your organization is interested in impact, an attractive market might be one where your work contributes to saving lives. It all depends on what your organization is aiming to do, and is a matter of judgement. The assessment could look something like:

Product	Market attractiveness	Score	Justification
Instrumentation	◄ ▮ ►	24	Small market
Training services	◄ ▮ ►	19	Many low price competitors, medium market
Consumables	◄ ▮ ►	65	Large market but many competitirs
Consultancy	◄ ▮ ►	12	Small market competes with in-house staff
Reference materials	◄ ▮ ►	73	Niche market, few competitors

The second step is to score the organization's capability in the segment or group of products. Carrying out the analysis for a group of products is therefore usually easier than dividing the market by segment. This is again a difficult assessment, for example, your organization's expertise has to be scored relative to competitors. The assessment brings in information from previous steps in this process (i.e. you can't dive straight into this, you have to have done the groundwork). Typically, you would take into account issues such as:

- The expertise and experience your organization has
- Resources available — equipment, facilities, access to raw materials
- Cost base
- Accreditations held/patents held

Again, you will need to score your organization's capability (out of 100), ending with an assessment that may look something like:

Product	Capability	Score	Justification
Instrumentation	◄ ▮ ►	85	Experience in construction, key patents
Training services	◄ ▮ ►	25	Expert staff but limited training experience
Consumables	◄ ▮ ►	14	Limited range available
Consultancy	◄ ▮ ►	73	Experienced staff
Reference materials	◄ ▮ ►	79	Comprehensive range

The next step is simply to plot the market attractiveness versus your organization's capabilities:

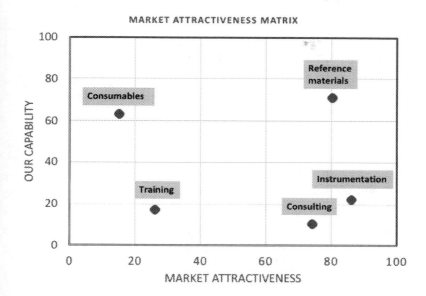

The position on the matrix will give you some indication of what you should do about a product (or a segment, if you have decided to split the analysis that way). Broadly, the matrix can be divided into four sections:

- Low market attractiveness, low capability — consider exiting?
- Low market attractiveness, strong capability — what can be done to make the market attractive?
- Attractive market, low capability — what do we need to do to improve?
- Attractive market, strong capability — how do we keep it this way?

At this point, you will find that the discussions will begin in earnest! Some pet products will suddenly look not quite so attractive to your organization, but that is the point of this analysis.

Outputs from this stage

- An analysis of which parts of the market are attractive with some justifications, taking competitors into account
- An analysis of whether your organization is in a good position to access the attractive markets
- Probably — a list of where you should invest, and where not
- A plot that gives a quick overview
- A paragraph or two summarizing the analysis

3.4 Ansoff Matrix

This is a very simple but useful diagram that summarizes the products and customers to develop the strategy for the organization. It shows what actions you could take, and it also shows the risks. One application of it is to balance what you are doing, so you don't put all your eggs in one basket — it is all too easy for scientists to want to work on the new technology and to leave the existing products to wither on the vine.

It is very simple to use. You divide up your product range into four categories as shown in the diagram below:

This approach is easy to adapt for scientific research: for 'existing products' read 'well-known science', and for 'new products' read 'new research fields'. However it is interpreted, the Ansoff matrix leads to four main questions:

Existing products, existing customers: *What do we need to do to consolidate our position, to ensure that at least we retain these customers?*

This is of course the least risky category. Even so, it is worth putting in some serious effort to retain the customers. The focus is probably on ensuring effective communication with customers to demonstrate that you are still in business, but you may have to consider what is happening to prices in the market and what your competitors are doing. There may also be opportunities to ensure that your customers increase how much they use your existing products.

Within your organization much of the scientific research has been completed, but it should not be neglected, otherwise there is a risk that competing organizations will move ahead.

There is, of course, a downside to adopting this strategy from the point of view of scientists working in the laboratories. It's reasonable to assume that it should be possible to learn how to carry out the work more efficiently as there are no changes going on, so there will be continual pressure to reduce costs — reduce investment in equipment and reduce staff. This may explain why sometimes you see investment going elsewhere in the organization.

Existing products, new customers: *How do we increase the number of customers that use our products?*

This is more risky, as you have to bring new customers on board. For many products, this could involve expanding geographically, moving into different regions or different countries.

But in science and engineering, this is a very interesting category to consider. Many developments in science happen on the boundary between different scientific disciplines, and bringing your product to market is the same challenge. For example, does your product, which was developed to solve a problem in the oil and gas industry, also have a potential application in the nuclear industry? This is where the information you gathered for the political, economic, socio-cultural, and technological analysis (PEST analysis) can come in very useful.

With this category, there is an emphasis on finding potential new customers, and then promoting the existing product range, maybe changing the message you are communicating to appeal better to them.

New products, existing customers: *How do we build on our links with our existing customers?*

This is also riskier than simply consolidating your existing product range with your customers. What new products are your customers asking for? Can an existing product be adapted or additional benefits added? Can new services be developed (for example, training services to support an existing product?

New products, new customers: *Can your organization diversify?*

The riskiest approach of all, but also the category that feels the most attractive to innovative scientists and engineers. In addition to finding potential customers, actions include adapting your products to match the new market.

In summary, the Ansoff matrix helps you decide what actions your organization could take:

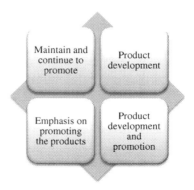

Outputs from this stage

- An assessment of where investment is needed, and whether it is on promotion or product development
- A simple graphic that shows the risk
- A paragraph or two summarizing the assessment

3.5 Summary — Your Organization's Mission and Vision

In this section, we have covered three tools from professional marketing that you could use to analyze the information you gathered. You may have come to the same conclusion we did — they are useful and act as a framework to structure a conversation, and possibly you will have had some useful insights.

You have a good idea of where your organization sits in the market and what you are aiming to do. Now is probably the time to write down two statements that summarize your organization — the mission statement and the vision statement. The mission statement says what the organization wants to do now, the vision statement says what it wants to do in the future. Both statements should be concise, clear and inspirational (the latter of course being the most difficult to achieve).

A good mission statement will cover:

- What do we do today?
- Who benefits?
- For what reasons?

Here (adapted for the purpose of this book) is the mission statement for a government-funded programme the authors were involved in: 'Our mission is to ensure ionizing radiation can be used effectively for cancer therapy, through enabling medical physicists to quantify patient doses at an accuracy that is fit for purpose'. It is not particularly elegant, but was clear enough for people working in the field at the time and it captured what the organization would focus on.

A good vision statement will:

- Describe what we hope to do in the future
- Set out our realistic aspirations
- Describe an outcome
- Use no business jargon
- Be enthusiastic

A good vision statement also distinguishes your organization from others in the field and should be short, simple and memorable. Microsoft's vision statement, *There will be a personal computer on every desk running Microsoft software*, is perhaps a very good example.

Writing these statements is really a way to test yourself on the analysis. They should be very easy to write; if they aren't, it is worth reflecting on why you find it difficult — what have you missed?

Following the information gathering and the analysis, the next step of course is to decide what actions to take. There are tools from marketing to help this process as well, and that is the topic of the next section.

Chapter 4

Deciding the Actions to Take

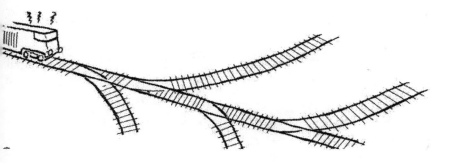

In this chapter:

- Tools for communication with your stakeholders

- How to decide prices to charge

- How to make it easy for your stakeholders to work with you

- Dealing with intellectual property issues

- The types of product you could offer

4.1 The Marketing Mix

Having gathered information on the market and worked your way through some analysis exercises, the next phase is to work out what your organization will actually do. To be effective, the diverse actions will need to work in harmony.

Marketing professionals refer to the 'marketing mix'; a summary of the most important factors to consider. It suffers from the awful description of '4Ps and an S' as no one has come with a better acronym. In essence, to build a consistent plan you have to consider five different elements:

(1) Promotion (communication with the customer)
(2) Price (the cost to the customer)
(3) Place (how convenient it is for the customer to work with you)
(4) Product (what benefits will the customer get)
(5) Service (what back-up services you offer)

We'll look at each of these elements of the marketing mix in turn, with a focus on 'Promotion' and 'Product' as these are the most likely aspects that a scientist will be drawn into.

4.2 Promotion: Communicating with Your Customers

All the analysis has really been leading up to this: devising a plan to communicate with your customers. You may be trying to win business or you may be trying to persuade other organizations to adopt your ideas — whatever the reason, the communication will be much more effective if you take the time and trouble to plan communications with your customer.

Taking part in an industrial exhibition will showcase your products, but sending potential customers an email ahead of the exhibition with the benefits of your new instrument, writing an article for a trade journal, then taking part in the exhibition and having a plan to follow-up afterwards is much more likely to have the desired effect.

The problem is that selling is a multi-dimensional problem: lots of factors are to be taken into account all at the same time. In no particular order, it's important to consider:

- What methods do you have to communicate with your customers
- How do you balance long-term strategic actions with short-term tactical actions
- How do you match the communication to the customers
- Whether it is a new product or it has been on the market for a long time
- How people buy

We'll look at each of these in turn, before putting everything together into a communication plan.

4.2.1 *Methods to Communicate with Your Customers*

There are, of course, the usual ways to communicate with customers that any organization can use — targeted emails, the website, blogs, articles in trade journals, advertisements, sales visits, stands at trade shows and telesales. Perhaps, even mailshots can be useful — rarely used these days but they have the advantage that they are not blocked by firewalls (an important issue if your customers are in the defence sector or other security-sensitive organizations).

We are very fortunate in science in that we have other powerful tools at our disposal. We're good at using these tools — it is what we are trained to do:

- Presentations at scientific conferences
- Papers in scientific journals
- Running technical training courses
- Running proficiency test exercises or demonstrations of methods
- Writing application notes or good practice guides

These are all examples of how the communication with the customer has some intrinsic value to the customer. One of the authors was looking for an asbestos measurement company to help with a project; the author knew nothing about asbestos (and only wanted to know enough to complete the project), so the company that published a short summary of the regulations and the technical issues was the organization that was contacted. It probably also saved them time — the author was able to speak to them with at least a vague understanding of the field.

Finally, word of mouth can be a very important tool in the scientific field. This is particularly powerful if what your organization is offering is very complex so communicating every aspect would be impossible to do and very difficult for the customer to evaluate. The confidence that someone else, respected in the field, has adopted what your organization offers can be invaluable. Of course, you can't control 'word of mouth', but your organization can help to influence it by involving key individuals in development of the project, giving them a reason to show off ('Of course they only added that feature after they had spoken to me').

The message from this section is: write down a list of all the ways you could communicate with your customers in your field. You may be surprised.

4.2.2 *Strategic Versus Tactical Actions*

The snag with doing what we are good at (presentations at conferences, papers, etc.) is that it doesn't bring in the customers. Perhaps people at the conference will listen politely to your proposed new method or the description of the new instrument, but it is very passive. If you are honest, how many new ideas presented at conferences have you put into use in your organization?

Such communications are about positioning your organization, persuading the audience that your organization is good to deal with. It could be telling them about the high quality of your work or the ingenuity of your scientists. Any effect on sales is more in hope than expectation (if your boss

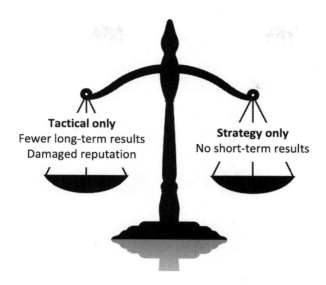

asks you 'if you go to the conference and give the presentation, what sales will you bring back with you?', it's probably worth investing some time updating your CV). The communications are strategic in nature — they have a long-term impact — but you need other actions to bring in the sales or persuade the stakeholders to adopt your proposals. They can generally get attention and perhaps interest from customers, but there it will stay.

So you also need the shorter term, tactical actions, to close the sales. Face-to-face selling by a trained sales force is of course the obvious communication tool to use, but it is expensive. Telesales is cheaper, but generally results in a very bad-tempered former customer (rarely used in science except for people selling attendance at very expensive conferences). Very closely targeted mailshots, or free product training sessions, can be used. This is what Sales and Marketing Departments are good at.

However, concentrating on the tactical actions alone means that your organization will eventually get the reputation of being only interested in the money. Very few scientists joined the profession because they were motivated by money, so this is not a good reputation to get. The trick is to balance the strategic and tactical actions, to keep the organization's reputation but also bring in the essential sales. It can mean scientists working closely with Sales and Marketing, and it can pay dividends.

4.2.3 *The Product Lifecycle*

The promotional plan also depends on what stage your product is at in what's called the product lifecycle. There are three key stages — growth, maturity and decline.

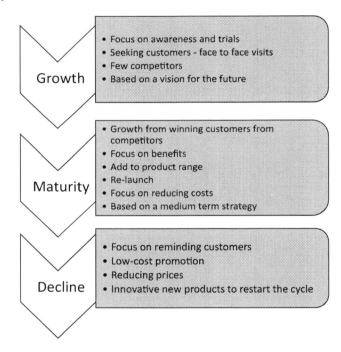

4.2.3.1 Growth

The first stage in the lifecycle is of course launching the new product onto the market. This is the exciting stage, when efforts are concentrated on telling potential customers and hopefully the first sales start to come in (so-called early adopters). There are also usually very few competitors, and key messages can concentrate on the benefits of the product. It is also the most risky stage, and it needs visionary management to stick to the plan despite the inevitable early setbacks.

Research has shown that there are five key factors that help the success of launching a new product[a]:

- Very clear benefits to the user
- Familiar to the user — easy for the user to see how it can be used
- Simple — the 'I-wish-I'd-thought-of-that' product
- Easy to trial the product
- Easy to see the results of others using the product

In the science sector, the last two factors are easy to address — organizing on-site demonstrations or training on new instruments, using industrial exhibitions, inviting potential customers to your organization to see it in use, etc. If you are very cheeky (and there are suppliers that do this!) you can even get away with charging customers to attend the training session by adding other material to the course. Seeing others using the product is also straightforward — scientific papers referring to its use or perhaps offering substantial early discounts to key, high-profile, organizations (on the condition that the product can be used for training).

The other factors can be more difficult, and the art of writing good marketing material kicks in at this point.

4.2.3.2 Maturity

Once the product is established on the market, competitors will join in (even if you have patent protection, different approaches to solving the customer's problems may be found). From a sales or impact point of view, the aim is to win back the sales from competitors. This is a period of incremental additions to the product, adding new features or services, and sometimes relaunching the product to remind people of you. On the plus side, it should be possible to develop a robust medium-term promotional plan to work to. Management attention turns to making the product or running the service efficiently, getting rid of the 'nice to haves' that have crept in.

---

[a]Chris Rice, *Consumer Behaviour: Behavioural Aspects of Marketing.* Butterworth-Heinemann, Singapore, 1993.

4.2.3.3 Decline

All good things come to an end, and at this point in the product life cycle it has become a commodity. There are probably lots of competitors selling similar products and it becomes increasingly difficult to distinguish one from another. Reducing the price is probably the only approach to maintaining sales volume.

Cost saving is therefore the name of the game — continuing to promote the product by using cheaper methods (the website rather than the sales force, for example) and looking for ways to reduce costs in-house. Management attention turns to the next new product and the cycle starts again.

4.2.4 *Matching the Message to the Customer*

Even within a market segment, there will be basically four types of customers:

- Those who have never heard of your organization
- Those who have heard of the organization and like dealing with it
- Those who have heard of the organization, and don't really have an opinion about it
- Those who have heard of the organization and are negative towards it

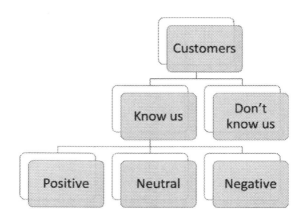

The style and content of communications have to be tailored to how your customers view the organization. If they've not heard of you, you will need something bold and impactful to catch their attention, and a promotional plan that is weighted towards strategic actions may be the way to go. An approach like this would bore your existing positive customers, so a promotional plan for them would be biased towards tactical actions.

The most difficult group to address is those who are negative towards the organization. They may disagree on an intellectual level with what your company is offering, they may have had a bad experience when dealing with the organization and harbour bad feelings, they may even have a predisposition to dislike your organization (for example, strongly held ethical views that your organization doesn't appear to match). Whatever the mix of emotional and logical views, the message has to be thought about very carefully. Bold, impactful techniques are likely to annoy them, just as much as more direct tactical approaches. It is very difficult to change attitudes, and the best you can do is to keep your messages positive, and keep them clear, relevant and repeated. (This is not the case of course if you are dealing with a complaint — staying positive gives the impression that you are not listening, which rarely goes well.)

In all of these cases, it is important to think about what your organization is offering the customer from the customer's point of view. The message should emphasize the benefits to them of your product or service; one way to check you are doing this is to ask yourself 'so what?' as you write down a description of the product (what is the value to them — the 'value proposition'). It should also emphasize what is different compared to your competitors, but again making sure that it is from the customer's point of view, not yours. Examples of how other organizations have used the product and benefited from it are useful, linking the message to something that is relevant to the customer may also be useful (e.g. 'reference materials for annual calibration to meet regulations' may be more effective than just 'calibration materials').

Approaches to engage customers may work — something that perhaps puzzles the customer until they read further.

4.2.5 *How People Buy — A Simple Model*

The very first sales promotion one of the authors devised was a complete flop. They had been introduced to some products used to calibrate spectrometers, widely used in Germany but never adopted in the UK. The products seemed to have strong advantages over the UK approach (for a start, they didn't potentially leak radioactive materials over laboratories and staff if you dropped them). So a flyer was devised, posted (no email then!) to potential customers and we waited for the sales to roll in. Which of course they didn't: amongst other factors, the campaign didn't consider how people go about buying.

Research on the process used by people to decide to buy your product or to adopt the technology you are proposing would fill a library. The first lesson every sales person is taught is that you have to lead the customer through a process of understanding the product logically and then deciding to buy, which is more of an emotional decision that would meet the eye.

Every single sales person you meet will therefore know the acronym 'AIDA'. There's nothing much to back up that it works, but it does at least give you a framework to think about in planning a promotional campaign and it is easy to remember. The way it works is this:

Attention: The first step is to cut through the noise to grab the attention of your customer. Perhaps it is an image on your exhibition stand that makes it stand out relative to your competitors. Using words like 'New' or 'Free' have also been shown to get attention.

Interest: Once you have their attention, the next step is to engage the logical part of the brain. Showing how the technique or product can be used, spelling out the key benefits. Something to intrigue the customer.

Desire: The customer may be interested, but it is an emotional decision to actually place the order. The sales person 'helps' the customer by emphasizing the benefits and perhaps pointing out what will happen if they don't purchase the product or adopt the new approach (this is called 'increasing the gap').

Action: Finally, you have to tell the customer how to place the order. It's worth remembering this step — flyers on local events where the writer has forgotten to say where the event is taking place are all too common.

AIDA can be used at many levels — from devising a promotional plan for a major product launch, to trying to get the new technique you have developed adopted, to designing a web page or a flyer.

4.2.6 *Devising a Communication Plan*

There are therefore many different issues to take into account — devising a good promotional plan is not easy. Different communication tools are useful as you take the customer through from 'attention' to 'action', and the tools can be used in different ways.

Method	Strategic		Tactical	
	Attention	Interest	Desire	Action
Website		x	xx	
Conference talks	xx	xx	x	
Application notes		x	xx	x
Sales visits		x	xx	xx
Advertisements	x	x		
Articles in journals	x	x	x	
Telesales				x
Scientific committees	x	x		
Emails		x	x	x
Training courses		x	x	x
Industrial exhibitions	x	x	x	x

Note: x = may be best suited to this stage, but it will vary from industry to industry.

Some of these tools are particularly useful in the scientific field, and the next sections include some points you may wish to bear in mind.

4.2.6.1 Industrial Exhibitions

'I think we should book a stand at the exhibition later this year' are words that strike fear into the heart of any scientist who has helped colleagues run a booth at an industrial exhibition. Industrial exhibitions are ideal opportunities to meet potential customers and stakeholders for your products and services — they are often attached to scientific conferences attended by your peers — and so are a very common tool for promoting scientific products and services.

All too often though, running a booth can be an expensive mind-numbing experience during which you regret deeply not wearing more comfortable shoes. So, here is some guidance on how to make the experience useful (there's no underpinning theory or studies for this guidance, just experience from many mistakes the authors have made over the years — it's common sense but it is surprising how uncommon sense is at times).

4.2.6.1.1 Selecting the exhibition

There is a huge number of scientific conferences and associated exhibitions in all fields of science. They can range from small local conferences focused on a specific group of potential customers to more general scientific conferences. The focused conference can be cost-effective, but you have to be sure that the delegates really are your potential customers (checking which other organizations are also exhibiting can be a good way to be sure that the conference is relevant). The larger exhibitions will obviously have a wider range of delegates, but will be more expensive and the booth will need to look very professional to stand out. Only experience in your particular field will tell you which are the good conferences for you and which should be avoided.

Don't forget to check the language that the conference is in and who is likely to attend! Some organizers advertise in English and call the conference 'international', but it is held in the local language and if you have no one who can speak the language, you are lost. It really does happen, to the amusement of other exhibitors — all you can do is make the best of a bad job, abandon the stand and go sightseeing. Fortunately, for one of the authors, Barcelona is a very nice city to visit.

4.2.6.1.2 Selecting the position of the booth

The position of the booth in the exhibition hall can make a significant difference to the number of visitors. Most exhibition organizers will send you a plan of the hall and offer a choice of locations, but without seeing the exhibition hall, it can be quite tricky to select a good position. At the ends of aisles, clearly visible to conference delegates as they walk into the hall, or near the coffee point are popular choices and not down a side room (which sometimes happens — cheaper, but you won't see any delegates). Be careful when interpreting the plan, what looks like a great location at the top of the stairs on the plan can in fact be hidden. If in doubt, ask the conference organizer.

4.2.6.1.3 Laying out the booth

There are basically two ways you can design the layout of the stand. First, set up a table at the back of the exhibition booth with the products, brochures, etc., stand to one side and talk to customers who are interested enough to come into the booth. Alternatively, set the table up at the front of the stand and stand behind it, to talk to potential customers as they walk past.

You will need some eye-catching posters so that the delegates know which organization you represent as they wander past. When designing the posters, use 'AIDA' — something to attract attention, something to interest the delegates, something to make them want to come to talk to you. There is a bewildering variety of very clever fold-out stands and lighting systems available to mount the posters — it's worth investing in good quality stands as they tend to get battered during transport.

One tip to bear in mind — if you want delegates to take away a copy of your brochure, don't place them on the stand in a very neat pile as it puts people off taking a copy — make them look just a little bit untidy.

4.2.6.1.4 Attracting visitors

You obviously want visitors to your stand, but also you want the right visitors. The company that gave away a bottle of wine to everyone visiting their stand had a long queue, but few delegates had any interest at all in their products. There are other less expensive 'giveaways' you can have on the stand (pens, rulers, mouse mats, mugs, sweets, etc., all marked with the company logo), and you will get some delegates visiting the stand for these, but are equally too general to attract the right people.

So the challenge is how to add value to your stand, to bring the right people to your stand. Giving a presentation at the conference about your research (perhaps about a new technique or instrument you have developed), and then telling delegates you will be on the booth to answer any questions can be very effective. If you can't do that, making technical literature and training materials available can be useful.

However, by far the best way is if you know potential customers who will be attending the conference, invite them to meet you at a specific time at the stand. Some experienced exhibitors set aside an area of the stand with a coffee machine and table and chairs, so you can discuss the products in detail.

4.2.6.1.5 Practical arrangements

Invest in a set of robust packing cases for all the material you will need (posters, brochures, stands, instruments, etc.), but make sure they will fit into the van or estate car you are using. It is also wise to take a trolley, as it can be a long walk to the booth.

Pack a set of tools and miscellaneous items you might need to repair the stand or to put posters on the walls, etc. (scissors, pliers, adhesive tapes, pens, paper, fuses for the lighting system, spares for anything you can think of). Take good quality cloth, preferably in a colour that matches your organization's logo, to cover any tables you may want to use. The authors have spent many unhappy hours driving to the local shops to buy something needed to ensure that the stand looked good.

Most importantly, arrive in plenty of time. All the other exhibitors will be arriving at roughly the same time, and if you are late it will be impossible to park and you will end up dragging the exhibition material a long way, arriving flustered and rushed.

Be careful about local regulations (for exhibitions) for setting up the stand or plugging in the lighting. For example, some exhibitions in the USA insist that only the conference staff are allowed to do some activities when setting up the stand — if in doubt, ask the organizer.

Finally, if you are taking examples of instruments or products to another country, check that you have the correct paperwork in place to avoid the item being held up in customs. You will not be selling the instrument, etc. in the country so you should not have to pay customs duties, but you may have to prove this.

4.2.6.1.6 Sponsoring

You will without doubt be asked by the conference organizer if your organization would be prepared to sponsor the conference. This can range from paying for the wine at the conference dinner, to buying the conference bags, to sponsoring a session at the conference, all in exchange for a mention of your organization by the session chair, a copy of your logo on the conference programme or the inclusion of printed literature in the folder given to delegates when they arrive. The cost can range from a few hundred pounds to a few thousand, depending on the conference (with medical conferences amongst the most expensive).

It's very difficult to assess how effective sponsoring the conference is — the best you can hope for is to raise the awareness of your organization, so it could be useful if your organization is new to the field. It is basically a way for the conference organizer to help cover the costs of running the conference (they are very expensive and the delegate fees have to be kept low to attract enough attendees). The authors have experience of sponsoring conferences to get a negative return (in one case, the session chair just said, 'We've had to get this session sponsored by <organization>, so get your free T-shirts at the back' — not the company image we wanted to project). The best advice is to be very clear on exactly what you will get for your money (what prominence will your logo have — will it be lost in a sea of other logos? Will your organization be mentioned at the conference session or will the conference organizers simply take your money?).

One approach that the authors have found works well is to provide a prize for the best poster. This means that your organization gets involved with the conference organizers and leading scientists to judge the posters, it gets mentioned at the prize giving at the end of the conference, and positions the organization as supporting the science (which the delegates in general like).

4.2.6.1.7 During the event

First, appoint someone to be in charge of the stand — someone who will set up a rota for manning the stand, be the point of contact with the conference organizer and decide how to layout the booth.

Don't be afraid to change the layout of the booth. The received wisdom of having the instruments at the back of the stand so delegates have to walk in doesn't always work; it may work better if you set up the stand with a table at the front and you behind it. Experiment with the layout and see what works.

Talk to people who show an interest in the stand — don't wait for delegates to start talking to you. 'Hello, I don't think we've met, which organization are you from?', 'Have you heard of our organization?' Just be polite and interested in what they are doing at the conference, it doesn't matter if they have no interest in your products, just end the conversation politely. There are cultural differences to be aware of, though in the USA delegates will expect you to approach them to sell your products, in the UK they can be more reserved.

Keep very good records of anyone who has shown an interest in your products and services, as you will forget who they were a few minutes later. Pre-printed forms with a checklist you complete immediately after the delegate has left the stand are invaluable. Make sure you get their business card (don't expect them to contact you after the event, it is up to you to follow-up).

Every scientific conference has its fair share of eminent scientists who have made excellent contributions to the field over the years and are now semi-retired. They will never buy your products or services, but they influence others. The problem is that they are very happy to chat to you at the stand during the conference coffee breaks, it would be incredibly rude to cut them short but at the same time you can see people you really wanted to meet

- You tell the group that you would like a guest worker to join the group to work with them for a few weeks or months
- Your colleagues will grumble about the work needed to train the new person, that they will need constant supervision, and they will slow down the work
- The guest worker will join, will turn out to be a likeable human being
- The guest worker will make good progress on the project
- The guest worker will leave, having enjoyed the experience
- The guest worker will end up as a senior member of staff in their organization and will speak up for yours for many years to come

Why can we assume this will happen (apart from the authors' experience)? First, any organization sending a guest worker to yours is not going to choose someone who won't fit in and do a good job. Second, look at how well universities are expanding.

4.2.6.5 Collaborative Projects

Working on collaborative projects with other organizations is probably one of the best ways to communicate the results of the projects, to learn about what your customers need.

4.2.6.6 Use of the Internet

The use of the internet is an interesting one in the scientific world. There are obvious uses — as an easy access point for training materials, application sheets, links to scientific publications, technical data sheets, good practice guides, background information that may be useful to your customers, etc. Many companies selling laboratory consumables offer the possibility to order products directly online.

Here are some other ways the authors have used or seen for promoting science:

- Providing background technical information (historical background, for example) — apart from helping to build the credibility of your organization, such information is often picked up by lecturers looking for information for presentations helping to promote your organization.

- For those who can't attend a scientific conference, providing copies of presentations (subject to agreement from the presenters of course) or broadcasting the conference through the web — all helps to bring customers to your website.
- Short videos (on your website or on platforms such as YouTube). The authors have seen these used as ways to explain a change in the strategy of an organization and to demonstrate novel technologies such as a new robotic system. These can be very effective but also have to be very professional — we are scientists, not trained actors, and sometimes the videos just don't work very well.
- Providing some services directly, such as e-Learning packages.
- Building confidence in the capability of your organization by short summaries of the expertise of key staff, including their research interests and publication record (used very effectively in academia).

Many scientific organizations have an active presence on social media (such as Facebook and Twitter), as a way to promote news stories and to stay in touch with customers.

The challenge for your colleagues in IT is ensuring that your products come up high in the list when potential customers search on key terms. Local, well-known representation still has an important role to play.

There are some limitations for the internet in the scientific world. Some organizations (for example, those in the defence sector or the nuclear industry) restrict use of the internet, and customers cannot take advantage of the full capabilities. Some colleagues are reluctant to have any personal details online, and this has to be respected.

4.2.7 *Drawing This All Together — The Promotional Plan*

You have a wide range of tools available to you as a scientist to promote your work or help sell your products — all have their advantages and disadvantages. The most powerful way to use them is to develop a plan to promote your work; the plan would usually have the following elements:

4.2.7.1 An Aim

First, decide exactly what it is that you want to achieve. Is it to sell your existing products (in which case you can track sales), to launch a new product or to persuade a group of people (for example, the people funding your science) that what you are doing is valued.

4.2.7.2 The Segment (or Segments) You Want to Communicate with

For example, are you aiming at the scientists, the technicians, the management, the regulators, the general public?

4.2.7.3 A Message

What is the key message that you want to get across to the segment? For example, the message could be 'This new product will help you comply with the new regulation'. The message needs to be simple and aimed at the segment, and aimed at the benefits you think your customers are looking for, not the features you are trying to sell. 'What is in it for them' is the key part of the message.

4.2.7.4 A Way to Grab Attention (A)

First of all, you have to select one or more of the communication tools to grab the attention of your customers. It's probably easier to rule out the tools that won't work — updating the website won't do this.

4.2.7.5 A Way to Get the Customers Interested (I)

Having got their attention, the next step is to try to capture the customers' interest. The important part here is to emphasize the main benefits — how is it going to help them?

4.2.7.6 A Way to Get Your Customers to Want to Know More (D)

At this stage, you're trying to offer more and more information, so the website becomes a very useful tool, particularly if it has been updated to align with the earlier stages in the promotional plan.

4.2.7.7 A Way for the Customers to Act (A)

Finally, you want the customers to act on the information.

4.2.7.8 A Schedule

All of this work has to be scheduled so that the actions lead on from one to another.

No matter how complex it is, we hope we have convinced you that, as a scientist, you have a role to play in communicating with the customers and that you have the skills to do so. The next section looks at another aspect of the marketing mix — setting prices.

Outputs from this stage

- A promotional plan combining strategic and tactical actions
- A schedule

4.3 Setting Prices

If the aim of your organization is to sell products or services (or to bid for research projects), you may get involved in setting prices. Here is some guidance on how to go about this.

The maxim is 'charge what the market will bear'. But it all depends on what you are aiming to do in the short and long term, what the competitors are doing, what stage in the product life cycle your products are at — there are many different factors that have to be balanced.

There are five approaches you could use.

4.3.1 *Cost-Plus Pricing*

This is the simplest and most inward-looking approach. You estimate the total cost of your product or service, add a profit margin that depends on your organization's policy and that gives you the price to offer the customer. The approach can take into account market factors to some extent — the profit margin to apply is generally higher for industrial sectors such as pharmaceutical industry and lower for more engineering-based projects.

There may be difficulties because the financial models used to work out the cost (including overheads, etc.) are usually complex and very imprecise. They also tend to be an average across the organization, so if your work is largely desk based you still have to contribute to paying for the large laboratory on the other side of the site. This can price you out of the market if you are not careful. One way to get out of this trap is to make an argument based on marginal costs — how much extra will it really cost your organization to carry out the work.

It can also be very difficult to estimate the time needed and other costs needed. A detailed analysis ('bottom-up') will usually over-estimate the time and cost, as the tendency is to allow for a margin of error on each task or item and then add them all up. The 'top-down' approach (estimating the cost from previous projects) can have the opposite problem that risks are not properly accounted for as you will not have analyzed what is needed in detail. The best way is to try both approaches and apply some judgement.

Cost-plus pricing also has another potential long-term trap for the unwary. There can be a temptation to charge different prices to take account of small differences in what you are doing for different customers to ensure a consistent profit margin. Very quickly, the pricing structure becomes more and more complex, everyone forgets the rationale for the prices and chaos reigns. Simplicity really is the best approach.

4.3.2 *'Me Too' Pricing*

If there are existing competitors in the market, you set a price that is the same as theirs. If your organization is established in the market, has a reasonable market share and no particular advantage over competitors, this can be the way to go. The focus of your organization in this case may be on reducing costs to improve the margin, or to ensure that you can match competitors if they reduce their prices.

4.3.3 *Penetration Pricing*

With this tactic, you set a price which is noticeably lower than your competitors in order to win market share — even to the point that you make a short-term loss on sales. This may not be sustainable for the long term, but you would aim to increase prices gradually.

It may also be a useful tactic to introduce new products or services to the market, or perhaps customers who buy the product will also need other, more profitable, products from your organization (for example, selling an instrument at a loss in order to win more lucrative sales of the matching laboratory consumables or service contracts).

If the aim of your organization is more focused on impact — benefiting society in some way — but you still have to charge something to demonstrate the value, penetration pricing may be an approach to attract the early adopters. You may have to do this to change 'need' into 'want'.

It can be counter-productive though — setting a low price can give the impression of poor quality.

4.3.4 *Premium Pricing*

If what you are offering has benefits above and beyond what your competitors can offer, you may be able to charge a premium on the going market rate. It depends on what your customers really value, what is important to them. It can be a tangible benefit (such as the instrument you have developed has a higher throughput or lower cost of consumables that your competitor's) or an intangible benefit (such as your brand's reputation).

This is where the strategic aspects of promoting your work are very important — positioning your organization in the market as the best in the business (rather than the cheapest, although this is of course also a reasonable strategy to follow). Charging a premium price helps to reinforce the message.

4.3.5 *Charge What the Value Is to the Customer*

Would that scientists could charge for the wider benefits their research brings! The theory is that the price should be related to the value of the work to your customer. Perhaps the main example of this in the scientific field is charging for maintenance contracts or for add-on features to large capital equipment, as it is very difficult for the customer to change the equipment. In most other cases, competitors will move in rapidly if there are high profit margins available.

So setting the price is actually quite difficult, you may have to have short-term and long-term pricing strategies, and the choice has to match the other aspects of the marketing mix.

Outputs from this stage

- A rationale for the prices charged, taking account of competitors
- A price list
- A paragraph or two summarizing the strategy and the reasons

---

4.4 Place

Somehow, you have to make it convenient for the customer to deal with you. This is particularly important for scientific products and services. Customers will need to see the new instruments, to learn the new techniques, etc., and this is difficult to do at a distance or in a non-native language (most scientists speak fluent English but are of course more comfortable in their native tongue).

The first challenge is to select the customers you wish to deal with — you could, for example, target a group of customers based on geography.

Then, consider how to make it convenient for this group to deal with you. Options to consider include:

- Setting up a local representative for your organization.
- Arranging a 'pop-up' presence near to your customers. It is possible to hire a temporary serviced office on many university campuses or on science parks, sometimes just for a week or two.
- Working hard on your internet site so that it acts as your local shop front — this will probably involve translating the content into the local language.

There are other practical factors to consider to make your organization convenient to deal with. The ownership of intellectual property is often an issue for scientific organizations, so legal departments have to be scrupulous in ensuring restrictive conditions are written into the terms and conditions of any contracts (and this is fair enough). The problem comes when flexibility is lost, and sales or use of your product are held back while legal departments argue amongst themselves — we've seen this process drag on for months, by which time a more flexible competitor has moved in and the customer has given up.

Behind the scenes of providing convenience to your customers there can, in many cases, be the infrastructure that enables your organization to supply goods or services across national boundaries. In the scientific world, this can be very challenging as it can involve shipping hazardous materials or instrumentation that are intended for civilian use but sometimes have military applications (for example, such 'dual-use' products in the EU require authorization from the government). In some cases, you need qualified personnel to pack the materials and sign the documents on behalf of your organization. The regulations are extremely complicated and are outside the scope of this book. It is your organization's responsibility to ensure compliance — ignorance is of course no defence — professional advice is essential.

Outputs from this stage

- A list of the actions needed to make your organization convenient to deal with
- A paragraph or two summarizing the approach and the reasons

---

4.5 Products

As a scientist, you are also likely to be heavily involved in this element of the marketing mix. The aim of this step is to think carefully about what your organization offers to customers, to identify any changes you will make and plan the development of new products. The Ansoff matrix is the basis and the matrix is in turn based on the information you gathered in the first stage — you will get many ideas for new products as you work through this part and the Ansoff matrix tells you what to concentrate on.

First of all, make a comprehensive list of what your organization offers, for example:

Products	Instrumentation Lab consumables
Services (paid)	Consultancy Calibration Analysis Training Mathematical modelling Auditing
Services (impact)	Technical advice Training Scientific articles Good practice guides Contributions to national and international standards
Intellectual property	Licenses Designs

The next step is to think about how your customers use your products. There is a much-told example given on marketing courses about why customers buy drills (the colour perhaps? the brand? the number of power settings?). The point of the example is that customers don't want a drill at all, they want holes in walls. What's important is the benefit (the 'value proposition' in marketing jargon if you prefer six syllables when three will do) and this can be difficult to define for scientific R&D.

It can be helpful (particularly if the aim of your organization is impact rather than selling products) to draw up an 'outcome relationship model' — a diagram that shows how your products/services lead to the benefits that your customers want. A simple example is shown below, with the benefits to the customers (intermediate benefits and what they really want in the end) on the right hand side:

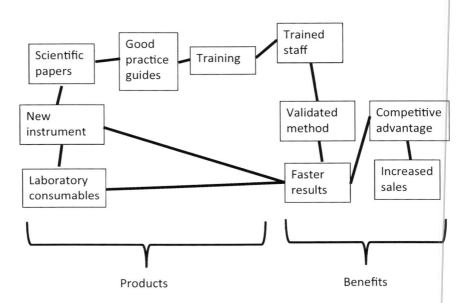

Armed with this model, the list of your products plus the information gathered on what your competitors offer, the next step is to discuss your product range. Questions to answer include:

- Should you modify your products, so that they could provide additional benefits for your customers?
- Are there any old products you could re-launch?
- Should you change the quality of some of the products? (Improving quality, or decreasing quality so the cost to your customers is lower)
- Should you offer customized versions of your products?
- Can you change the appearance of the product or its packaging? (This may seem trivial, but how do you feel if you spend £400 on a pair of glasses and they are delivered in a cheap case worth 50p?)

- Are you missing any products that could fill any gaps in the model?
- What products should you drop from the range?

There are three main risks to be aware of when proposing new products though. There is a risk of confusing customers by having too many different products, a risk of putting too much pressure on the operations staff to support a wide product range, and a risk that a new product can steal sales from an old product with zero (or negative) benefit to your own organization.

The next challenge is to identify any innovative products, new ideas that have the potential to create a new market or to change an existing one. Ideas can come from many different sources:

- Colleagues in other parts of your organization (including your sales force)
- Trade partners, end users, suppliers
- Scientific conferences and publications
- From studies of the segments and competitors

Ideas can also come by analyzing in great detail how customers use the products, and discussing which parts of the process could potentially be combined or split up with some benefit to your customers using your new product.

Scientists, being very creative, will have many ideas for new products. After consulting the Ansoff matrix to decide where the priorities lie, you will still have to take account of the fact that very few new products survive contact with the real world. Your organization will probably have a formal screening process to sift through the ideas for new products but, before enduring this, a simple tool (the Schrello screen) is useful so that at least you know the answers to some of the questions you will be asked. The Schrello screen challenges you to answer three simple questions — is it real, can it win and is it worth doing.

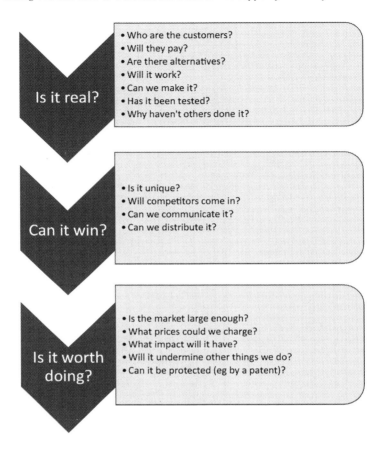

Once you have worked through this section, you will have a list of actions you need to carry out to implement — some will be under your control, some you will have to discuss with others in your organization.

4.5.1 *Intellectual Property Issues*

No book on the impact of science would be complete without at least some guidance on protecting your intellectual property. It is a key issue in science and technology, and the authors cannot emphasize strongly enough that it is important to seek advice from suitably qualified colleagues in your organization or one of the specialist patent companies if you have any intellectual property that could have some value.

Here is a very simple illustration of why professional advice is important. Let's say your organization makes coloured shapes, it has just developed a red square and wishes to protect it from competition by obtaining a patent. Your organization decides it wants to make the patent slightly more general, so files an application containing the following text:

'An object, wherein the object is a square, a circle, or a triangle, and wherein the object has a colour selected from red, blue or green.'

This wording would seem to cover the product and is more general to cover other possible products, so you might think it would be good enough. However, there can be subtle problems hidden away in the text. Suppose something published previously is found during the review process, and this 'prior art' discloses all of the possible combinations of shapes and colours, except for the red square. You would think that your application would still be OK — the red square hasn't been patented. Obviously, the claim now has to be amended, because otherwise it includes the prior art and lacks novelty, but patent law (in Europe) does not allow you just to delete 'circle', 'triangle', 'green' and 'blue'. The original wording includes two lists; making selections from multiple lists is regarded as creating new combinations of features not disclosed in the original document, and you are not allowed to add subject matter to a patent application after it has been filed.

In this simple example, your original application includes prior art, so it lacks novelty and the application is invalid. If the application is amended to remove the items covered by prior art, the application is also invalid because the amended application now includes added subject matter. A simple problem with the wording means that your patent application was doomed to fail from the beginning, and there is nothing you can do to rescue it.

Patent applications therefore have to be crafted with a great deal of care. The law can be very unforgiving and use rules that can seem contrary to common sense. It really is best to leave the legal aspects to the experts, as intellectual property is a complex area of law. However, intellectual property is probably the most important 'product' that a scientist can develop, so in this section we'll give a very brief overview of the topic (based on current European law).

4.5.1.1   Why Might It Be Worth Patenting Your Product or Idea?

The first approach that comes to mind when seeking to protect your intellectual property is of course applying for a patent. A granted patent gives an absolute monopoly over a claimed invention in a particular territory for a fixed period. The proprietor of the patent has the right to seek damages from anyone who infringes the patent by exploiting the invention commercially.

However, in exchange for the monopoly, the invention is made public and competitors will be able to use the invention once the time period has expired. Sometimes a patent is not the best way to go — keeping the know-how confidential and within your organization can be a good strategy; it just depends on the aims of your organization, exactly what the invention is, and what risk you're prepared to take (no patent = no legal protection).

That said, holding the exclusive right to exploit a particular product or process can be a significant advantage. Patents are assets, and can be sold (assigned), licensed or mortgaged, so may add value to your organization. Licenses can be granted for other organizations to use patents, and may be useful in negotiations with other organizations. Finally, patents can be a way for funding bodies to measure how innovative your organization is — if the patent application gets through the rigorous assessment process, it can be a huge 'tick in the box' for your organization.

Of course, the system can work the other way round for your organization. Ignorance of a patent is normally no defence and your organization can inadvertently infringe a patent and end up on the wrong side of a court case. Before bringing a new product or a new process to the market, it can be worthwhile to carry out a clearance search to check for any pre-existing patents.

4.5.1.2 What Can Be Patented?

This is a difficult question to answer. In principle, patents are available in respect of any invention, in any field of technology — the invention must be new and involve an inventive step. In Europe, the term 'invention' is not defined but the law does list some things which cannot be patented. The list is very narrow though, and again it is worth seeking professional advice.

Patents are available even for relatively small improvements, but there must be 'an inventive step'. Even finding an alternative way of achieving a particular effect may provide an inventive step. If the step is obvious to other scientists working in the field though, a patent application will be refused (in the legal jargon, the claim for an inventive step will be denied if the invention 'follows plainly or logically from the prior art') — there has to be something surprising, a step change, that the invention brings.

In addition to protecting the idea itself, other aspects of intellectual property can be protected — the brand or aesthetic aspects of a product, for example, can be protected.

4.5.1.3 What Must You Avoid Doing If You Are Thinking About Patenting Your Invention?

Here's where all too many scientists go wrong — many scientists are naturally excited by their invention and want to share their ideas with their colleagues. The problem is that you can only patent a new (or 'novel') invention if it has not been made public in any form before the date that the patent application was filed. Publishing the invention in a scientific journal, in a PhD thesis, giving a presentation at a conference, publicizing the idea on a website — all of these (and more) mean that the idea is no longer novel and you will not obtain a patent.

There are some exceptions though. If you have disclosed your invention without meaning to, act quickly and inform your patent advisor of the situation. They will need to know what was disclosed, and under what circumstances. Some territories, notably the United States, may disregard disclosures originating from the inventor when considering novelty. The European system allows disclosures which are made without consent, in breach of confidence, to be overlooked if a strict time limit is respected.

Disclosing the invention privately, in confidence, does not remove novelty. This is why your legal department probably stops you talking to people outside your organization about your invention until you have a 'Non-Disclosure Agreement' in place (if you don't have a legal department where you work, you can buy *pro forma* non-disclosure agreements on the web).

4.5.1.4 What Evidence Will You Need to Present?

An explanation of how and why the invention works can be all you need to put forward (particularly for simple mechanical devices).

Experimental data to back up your claims can be invaluable though, and make it much easier to establish the 'inventive step'. Even quite weak experimental evidence can be useful to your patent advisor — you only have to demonstrate that the effect you claim is plausibly achieved.

4.5.1.5 How Do You Apply for a Patent?

Applying for a patent involves filing an application, and then negotiating with the patent office over whether the application is allowable; the procedure to follow will be given on your local patent office website. The negotiation process is referred to as 'patent prosecution'.

To prepare an application and to arrive at an appropriate filing strategy, your advisor will need technical details regarding the invention and some indication of where patent protection will be needed. Let your advisor know if you plan to disclose (present, publish or even start to sell) the invention in the near future.

A patent provides protection only in the territory in which it is granted. A United Kingdom patent has no effect in the USA or Japan, for example. Protecting an invention in multiple territories requires multiple patent applications to be filed. There are ways to spread out the costs involved and your advisor will help you with this.

4.5.1.6 Why Might a Patent Application Be Refused?

Disclosing your invention before filing a patent application can be fatal to the application. Patent Examiners (or, indeed, anyone seeking to invalidate a patent) will search for prior publications by the inventors.

Prior art from other sources can be uncovered during the patenting process that may pose difficulties for demonstrating novelty or the inventive step. Prior art which is close to the invention can lead to failure on the ground that there is no inventive step, especially if the application includes little or no experimental data to support a favourable comparison with the prior art.

The technical content of the application may fail to provide an enabling disclosure of the invention leading to refusal on the grounds of insufficiency.

Adding subject matter to an application during prosecution is not permitted. It is imperative that the application is complete and correct on filing, as well as being structured in such a way as to allow for amendments to the application to be made. At least in Europe, the added subject matter provisions are applied extremely strictly.

4.5.1.7 What Do I Do If I Think Someone Infringes My Patent?

It is important to note that you will only have enforceable rights after your patent application is granted.

Do not contact a suspected infringer without obtaining advice first. Making threats of legal action relating to patent infringement can incur heavy penalties.

There are many options for dealing with infringement; your advisor will be able to provide guidance as to how best to proceed. Court action can be incredibly expensive. Often, the aim will be to reach some kind of amicable solution, such as a licensing agreement.

This part is therefore easy to summarize — if you are thinking of patenting your new product, please seek professional advice (the headline on the UK patent office website is 'Patents are expensive and difficult to get'). In the next section, we'll look at the next topic in the marketing mix — service.

Outputs from this stage

- Comprehensive list of your products
- Ideas for new products
- Outcome from an initial sift of ideas
- Probably, proposals to take forward for further evaluation
- A list of actions for yourself and colleagues
- A paragraph or two summarizing the findings

4.6 Service

The promotional plan concentrates on how you communicate with your customers or the people who will use the outputs from your work. The work doesn't stop there of course — you have to keep the contact going and make sure that you keep all the promises you have made to them. Your organization has to provide a back-up service of some form and check how well it is doing, and it is best to plan for this. As a scientist, your role can involve providing training, repairing instrumentation, advising customers, responding to complaints, etc.

4.6.1 *Providing Training for Customer Service Staff*

The first point of contact for your stakeholders and customers may be the people who work in the Customer Services Department (or a similarly named department). People in this role have a tough job — not only do they have to understand and use the organization's systems for order processing, they have to deal day-to-day with customers or stakeholders who expect them to understand all the jargon and to answer technical questions promptly and accurately. The same issues apply to distributors who may be representing your organization in other countries.

Effective training is important in supporting this work. Your role is often to train non-technical people about products and services — the key is to make this training interesting, fun, and non-threatening, at the same time as ensuring that training has been effective. Emphasizing the point of the products/research can be a good starting point (including some of the information from the studies of the market and customer needs) and using 'quizzes' to test understanding can be useful (for the quizzes, getting people to work in pairs or small groups makes it feel less like school, and also less threatening).

The promotional material pays dividends here as well. Material written for the website or brochures/catalogues can help reduce the number of technical questions that will come in, and can also be used as reference material by customer service staff. In fact, it is worth bearing this in mind when writing the material in the first place.

4.6.2 *After-Sales Service*

There can be two aspects to the after-sales service. First, there is the positive opportunity to contact your customer to sell laboratory consumables or other services, or to tell them about new ways they can use the outcomes from your research.

Second, less welcome, often overlooked and usually underestimated is the cost of repairing instruments that breakdown or providing time-consuming *ad hoc* technical advice. A simple risk assessment can be very useful at this point:

- Make a list of everything that could go wrong (don't forget about health and safety issues but bear in mind there are often regulations you must comply with as well, including the need to carry out a more sophisticated risk analysis than is described here — seek advice from your colleagues on this)
- Assess the probability of this happening as low or high, based on experience or on judgement
- Assess the impact if it does happen, again as low or high — again, it needs some justification about why you come to that conclusion

The next step is to determine what you could (and should) do to address each of the risks, putting most effort into the risks you have identified as 'high probability and high impact', followed by 'low probability and high impact', 'high probability and low impact' and finally 'low probability and low impact'. There may be several actions you can take, but actions normally fall into one of five categories:

Category	Type of action	Example
1	Do nothing	Log that there could be a risk of this happening and set up a system to log any feedback on this issue — then review whether inaction really is the best thing to do based on objective evidence.
2	Reduce the probability	Take steps to reduce something happening in the first place. For example, designing components to be more robust, testing the software extensively, providing training or advice to users to avoid this happening, etc.
3	Reduce the impact	Find ways to make the problem less serious. Perhaps, including spare parts with the equipment, training a local distributor to carry out the repairs, etc.

(Continued)

(*Continued*)

Category	Type of action	Example
4	Devise a contingency plan	Accept that it may happen, but have a plan in place to deal with it should it happen. For example, setting up an arrangement with a local organization to ship an instrument back to you for repair so that you are not rushing around to make the arrangements in a rush.
5	Insure against the risk	Pass the risk to an insurance company, so that you can claim back the cost of having to take corrective actions. Normally, though, this means assessing the cost to your organization and increasing the price so that you don't lose out should something happen.

What you end up with is a table summarizing the risk assessment:

Factor	Probability	Impact	Mitigation
Short description here	Low or High Short summary of justification	Low or High Short summary of justification	List here the actions agreed

4.6.3 *Responding to Complaints*

Most scientific organizations have their processes accredited to international standards such as ISO9001 or ISO17025. These standards require organizations to have procedures in place on how they are going to record and take corrective actions following complaints.

Your role in this is threefold:

- Responding quickly to any complaints that come in, answering any technical questions and finding solutions for customers. No one enjoys this part of the job, but complaints are inevitable and are best dealt with promptly rather than allowing the issue to fester.
- Helping to avoid the complaints in the first place. Carrying out a thorough risk assessment as part of the product development process and addressing any risks identified as important.

- Helping to design the complaint-handling procedure, to make it as efficient and effective as possible.

It is important to look on complaints in a positive way. They can be an opportunity — they can spark new ideas to improve your products or your research. They give you objective information on your organization's strengths and weaknesses to guide the analysis. They can, paradoxically, be an opportunity to build a stronger working relationship with the customer/stakeholder; dealing quickly and effectively with the complaint demonstrates to the person that your organization cares about them, and this can only be positive.

4.6.4 *Service-Level Agreements*

'If you can't measure it, you can't improve it'.[b] With this in mind, it can be very useful to discuss quantitative ways to assess the service you offer your customers and capture them in writing in a 'Service Level Agreement' (SLA). You can then track over time whether you are meeting what you set out to do and take corrective actions.

An SLA is not normally part of the legal contract when selling something — there may not even be a legal contract if your organization is supplying a public good — but it can sometimes be associated with a contract. The main differences between a contract and an SLA are usually that the contract can be enforced by law, the SLA is focused on service quality and is a measurement tool, and the SLA is much easier to change. An SLA is normally agreed in discussion with the customers, but can also be very useful as an internal process to self-assess how well your organization is doing (but in this case the detailed content will be very different from something you may wish to share with customers).

An SLA is therefore very flexible and typically covers:

- Who is responsible for what (for example, 'the Laboratory Manager is responsible for determining the metrics...')
- A list of the metrics (for example, 'the time taken between receipt of a technical question and the response')

---

[b] Attributed to the business guru Peter Drucker.

- The target (for example, '90% of technical questions will be answered within three days')
- Who will record what happens in practice (for example, 'the Customer Service Manager will collate the data on response times, using the date on the email with the enquiry and the date on the email with the response')
- How often this will be reported and what happens next[c] (for example, 'The Customer Service Manager will provide a summary of performance against the target once per quarter. The Laboratory Manager is responsible for reviewing the performance and taking corrective action if the target has not been met. Corrective action may include assigning additional staff to dealing with enquiries, updating the instruction manual, adding Q&A sections to the website ...')
- Any constraints
- Responsibilities on both sides (for example, 'The customer is responsible for providing the following information to facilitate analysis of the issue...')
- Timescales and responsibilities for reviewing the SLA itself (to ensure that it is kept current)

Outputs from this stage

- Training material for customer service staff and distributors
- Clear policy on after-sales service for maintenance and repair of instruments, etc.
- A risk assessment and list of actions arising
- Possibly, ideas for new products/services
- A list of actions for yourself and colleagues
- A paragraph or two summarizing the findings

4.7   Summary — Applying Product, Price, Place, Promotion and Service

The five elements of the marketing mix are interrelated and the aim is to be consistent. As one example of consistency, there is a category of

---

[c]There is no point in collecting the information if you intend to ignore it completely! It really is best to think through in advance what decisions might be taken.

product that is very common in the scientific world, which we will call a 'grudge purchase'. This is a product or service that an organization has to purchase in order to meet a regulatory requirement or an international standard, for example, an instrument and a technique to measure the amount of an impurity in a pharmaceutical or the quantity of radioactivity in waste materials. The organization does not make money from the purchase and it can seem to be simply an additional cost burden, but it is something the organization has to do and it wants it to be as easy to access and use as possible. The organization will only buy the product when it has to; no amount of negotiation from a charismatic sales representative will persuade the organization to place an order unless it must (perhaps due to old equipment breaking down or a change in the regulations).

On the other side of the fence, an organization that supplies these 'grudge products' therefore aims to

- Have a promotional plan that continually reminds potential customers that they are the best choice, so that they are the first supplier the organization turns to
- Work to keep prices low, with a clear pricing structure to make it easy for the customer to know what they will be paying
- Make it easy for the customer to access the products, through local distributors or a clear website
- Have innovative products that are easy to use
- Have a service to back up the products to make it easy for the customer

The '4 Ps and an S' work together to try to ensure that the customers receive a simple message: potential customers know where to purchase the product from, that the organization they are buying from has a good reputation, that it will be priced fairly and the whole purchasing process will be smooth and easy. The customer will appreciate not being contacted all the time to buy something they don't need.

Another example from the scientific world is bidding for research grants or large contracts. The systematic work you have done getting to this point will pay dividends. Most proposal forms ask you to explain the impact of the proposed research — your case will be much clearer and more powerful because you will be able to back up your assertions with reference to the stakeholders and customers who will benefit from the research and also how this links to the 'grand challenges' that you are aiming to address. In the sections where you are asked to describe your capability, you will be able to emphasize what makes your proposal different from possible competitors. You may have some information on prices your competitors may charge and you will be able to write all of this taking into account AIDA, to make your text compelling and easy for the assessors to read (which all helps). There is another advantage — you should be able to write bids much faster as you will not be searching for what to write at the last minute (and we can vouch for this being a good thing!).

Chapter 5

Recording the Analysis
and Reporting the Outcomes

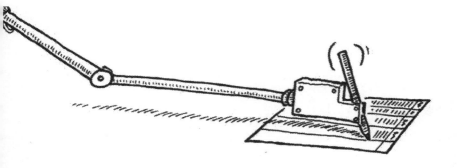

In this chapter:

- Advice on documenting the plans

- Approaches for seeking feedback from stakeholders

5.1 Reports

Most marketing plans we've ever seen end up in the dusty recesses of a computer drive, never to be seen again. Some end up as lengthy tomes with many multi-coloured charts. These documents have the same fate. The following year, the whole document is refreshed and filed again.

This makes no sense! The marketing plan needs to be an accessible document, pitched at different levels and easy to keep up to date. It also needs to be evidence based with easy access to the references used. One way we've found to do this is to use a structured database system (Microsoft OneNote® or similar software) to store the information, following the structure of the approach described in this book. It is easy to update, and you can include all the references in one place.

You will need a simple narrative though, that you can copy for use in other documents (for example, requests for capital funding or as the introduction to scientific papers), which summarizes the information from all the information gathering and analysis. We'd recommend avoiding the diagrams of market attractiveness, strengths, weaknesses, opportunities and threats (SWOT) analysis, etc. in the narrative — they are useful for presentations but, as we said before, it is the discussion that is important and it is easy to misinterpret a diagram without some sort of voice-over.

The following year, you can then add the new information and update the narrative, making it easy to maintain, rather than extensive re-writes.

5.2 Measuring Progress

Having invested a lot of time and effort in developing and implementing a plan to get the most out of your work, the next step is to find a way to check how well the plan is working, to enable you to refine the plan.

The metrics to choose depend on what your organization values. Looking back at the example of the benefit map (below), the commercial world tends to concentrate on measuring tangible financial results — measuring the sales, profit, return on investment, etc., and will concentrate on the right hand side of the benefit map. Academia will focus on the left hand side of the benefit map: the number of scientific papers published in prestigious journals, the number of citations, the number of patents filed,

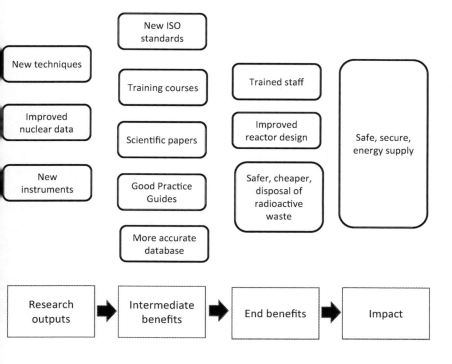

the additional funding that has been won to support the work.[a] Government-owned national laboratories are only too aware of the need to demonstrate the impact of their work, so that they can promote the value of their work to the politicians. However, in most cases, national laboratories try to avoid competing directly with commercial organizations, so will try to find quantitative measures for the intermediate benefits — closer to the end users than academia, but not directly related to sales.

5.3 Seeking Feedback

Getting feedback on scientific products and projects can be very challenging. There are several approaches you can try:

- Questionnaires, usually sent by email. The advantage of this approach is that it is very cheap to run. The trouble is very few people will bother to fill them in and you will mostly get complaints, but at least you will have an opportunity to try to deal with the issues that any end-users/customers may have. You can try to incentivise people to reply (e.g. by offering a free gift to anyone who responds), but the authors' experience is that it doesn't work very well in a business-to-business environment.

- Focus groups. The idea is that you invite a representative group of people to discuss how well your organization is doing — normally about 20 people. Some sort of structure is needed to get the discussions going — a series of questions. One risk is that discussions can be dominated by the handful of well-meaning but assertive people that work in all fields of scientific endeavour (you will know who they are in your field!) and you will miss valuable contributions from the quieter attendees. Skilled facilitation is therefore key and so some organizations hire professional facilitators to lead the meetings. The authors' experience is that this rarely goes well — very quickly focus group meetings descend into discussions of technical details, and a

---

[a] For example, Alex Ball, Monica Duke, 'How to Track the Impact of Research Data with Metrics'. DCC How-to Guides. Edinburgh: Digital Curation Centre. Available online: http://www.dcc.ac.uk/resources/how-guides, 2015.

facilitator with no knowledge of the field is rapidly reduced to asking delegates how to spell what they are talking about, to the frustration of all present. A better approach can be to ask people to discuss the topics in small sub-groups and then give feedback to the whole group (with of course some careful thought about who is in which sub-group). Focus groups can be very useful but tend to discuss day-to-day issues, and can be difficult to organize in a competitive industry where your customers may not wish to talk to each other.

- Governance panels. These can be much more successful — you invite a few key stakeholders to provide feedback on how well the work is going and what may be needed in the future. It will cost your organization some travel and subsistence for attendees, but many scientists enjoy the opportunity to meet their peers (and are even more likely to attend if you find a high profile Chair and call it a Governance Board).

Chapter 6

How to Use This Book

"No one learns as much about a subject as one who is forced to teach it."

Peter Drucker (management consultant and 'the founder of modern management'), 1909–2005

If you really want to apply the techniques in this book, the best way is to set out to teach your colleagues about them. In any case, the techniques described work best if your colleagues play a role in deciding what to do. Wherever you work, no doubt you will have attended strategy meetings, away-days, leadership team events and so on. You will have had reasonably meaningful discussions, probably leading to incomprehensible scribbles with pens that have almost run out on flip charts which you discuss at length in the hope that what your sub-group decides agrees with all the other sub-groups to avoid any risk of embarrassment. The flip charts are sometimes written up and thrown away, or (more honestly) just thrown away, and you go back to your day job, completely ignoring everything that was discussed. This is an utter waste of time, but organizations carry on doing this!

So here are some ideas on how to use the material in this book. What the authors have found works much better is to run workshops that are as close to normal working life as possible, to run the workshop differently at the different stages in the process, and not to try to do too much during each workshop. A few short workshops over a few weeks seem to work better than intensive away-days.

There will no doubt be some scientists taking part in the workshops who will be cynical about the value of following a structured process. Briefing such colleagues in advance of the workshops of the reasons and perhaps involving them in helping to run the workshops can help. If your colleagues are new to the approaches summarized in this book, the workshops may feel awkward at times but it is worth persevering. Little by little, it will become 'the way that things are done around here' and your colleagues will have adopted ideas from professional marketing without realizing that they have.

It is very important to establish an atmosphere of trust. The initial steps of gathering information on the market can help to build rapport as colleagues work together to collect and review the data. The more difficult part is the analysis, as everyone can have (and is allowed to have!) an opinion. The tools described try to make the discussions objective, but the facilitator will need diplomatic skills to keep everything on track.

The very first part is gathering information on the big picture — the long-term trends and societal needs that will impact your work. For a group new to this analysis, the easiest way we've found is for the person leading the work to identify the main stakeholders and print off copies of useful information from websites (reports, market overviews from professional bodies, etc.). After explaining what to look for in the reports, encouraging small groups to work together to build up the tables and draw the stakeholder map works well. The trick is to ask people to use their laptops or tablets to record the information or to search on the web for more reports (the printed copies give them an idea of what to look for) — it then feels more like day-to-day work than a separate activity.

Having sub-groups means that different perspectives are put forward for combination by the workshop leader into the summary document.

An alternative technique that can work well is to use a 'Delphi Exercise'. This technique was developed during the 'Cold War' in the 1950s as a structured method to consolidate knowledge from a group of experts, avoiding some of the interpersonal issues that can arise when experts disagree. For this technique, the facilitator draws up a simple questionnaire — each of the experts completes the questionnaire independently and returns it to the facilitator. The next step is for the facilitator to combine the answers into one document (this may be difficult but is easier to do than resolving disagreements between strong personalities in the middle of a meeting). This summary document is then sent to the experts for further comment and correction, and the process repeated if needed. The repeated drafting gives an opportunity for people to build on information from other experts. There is one ground rule for the exercise that is useful — all assertions must be supported by some evidence (e.g. references to peer-reviewed publications). This has two benefits: it tests what might be opinions and it gives a useful list of references that can be used for scientific publications.

The next steps (gathering information on customers and competitors) are easier as the information needed is well defined. If there are relatively few people at the workshop (up to about 10), it is straightforward for the facilitator to capture the information from colleagues in one session without having to split up into sub-groups and combine the data later (in fact, colleagues can get frustrated if sub-groups are simply duplicating work).

For these first three stages, you (as facilitator) will need to steer the discussion to get the information you need. Here is a list of open questions that you may find useful to adapt for your use if the discussions dry up:

Stage	Useful questions
'The big picture'	• What are government priorities? (for example, from publications, newspaper articles, speeches) • Which universities work in the sector — what are they doing (publications, conferences)? • Which national or international institutes? What are they doing? What review articles have they written and what do they say? • Which professional bodies are involved? What do their review articles say? • What new technologies could impact the field?

(*Continued*)

(Continued)

Stage	Useful questions
Customer analysis	• Which are the organizations that use the outcomes from your work? • Which departments do they work in? • Who exactly in the department? The laboratory managers? The research scientists? The technicians? • Put yourself in their shoes for a moment. What do they really want from us? Is it the same for everyone in the organization? • How do we know that? • What else might they want? • How many organizations are similar to this? • Is that number increasing or decreasing?
Competitor analysis	• Which organizations do what we do? • What products / services do they provide? • How large are they? How many research contracts do they win/how much do they sell? • What do they do to promote their work? What is their website like? What do they do at industrial exhibitions? • Are they more expensive or cheaper than us? • What would they do if we launch a new product? • Which of our customers are likely to take some of our work in-house? • Which of our suppliers might take over some of our work? • Any other organizations likely to move in? • What might put them off?

The next phase is to analyze the information (SWOT analysis, market attractiveness and Ansoff matrix). Dividing up into small sub-groups of four or five people gives more people a chance to contribute to the discussions and also allows the information to be looked at in different ways. The quantitative analysis can be done on paper, but it is easy to develop simple spreadsheets with 'sliders' for the scoring so that colleagues can concentrate on the discussion rather spending time working out the numbers. The spreadsheets can also be used as templates for recording the findings, avoiding the need for a lengthy write-up at the end. It really is surprising how well colleagues get engaged with the analyses (perhaps it is the objective nature of the methods that appeals to scientists?), and the exercises can lead to some vigorous discussions.

The analysis phase leads onto the more detailed planning and implementation phase. Workshops seem to be less effective at this point (too removed from the day-to-day work perhaps), and it seems to be more effective to work in small groups with those affected to devise the detailed plans, sort out the promotional material, etc. The phase is also likely to bring in more people from across your organization.

That brings us onto the difficult issue of pre-work — is it worth sending round briefing notes in advance of the workshops? It depends on how your organization operates, but the authors' experience is that no one ever completes any pre-work for any workshop, colleagues are busy enough as it is, and asking can be counterproductive. It is better to have a few slides explaining the background and reasons for the workshop at the beginning, but keeping it very short.

Most business-skills workshops provide some written material at the end as 'aide-mémoires' — copies of the slides perhaps with some notes, or short booklets. In the authors' experience, these are again filed and forgotten. It's more effective to give out a copy of a relevant book, it's much more likely to be kept and referred to later.[a]

One last piece of advice, if we may — don't give up! Some of your colleagues will find thinking about the customers or what society wants from their work very challenging — the culture in scientific research is sometimes valuing only scientific excellence, valuing the impact of the work on society as well may need a change in one's point of view. One of the authors' proudest moments was when a colleague who had been steadfastly arguing against the need for their work to have value for society, started to put their work into context, helped to steer the development of the strategy and their career started to take off.

---

[a]This is genuinely not a plug for more sales of this book — simply an honest account of the authors' experience!

Chapter 7

The Last Word

For your science to have an impact on the world (whether it is through developing new products and selling them, or making a contribution to addressing some of the grand challenges facing society), you have to plan for it. Adopting aspects of best practice from marketing gives you a framework for your plans, starting with researching the background for your work through to concrete plans you can implement.

The whole process is interactive, working with colleagues inside and outside the organization. Like science, it is also creative — taking basic principles and applying them to the issues your organization faces and inventing new approaches, new ways to communicate with the people your work is intended to help.

We hope that we have convinced you that, as a scientist, you have a role to play in selling your science and, above all, it is a role that you will find enjoyable and rewarding.

Bibliography

There are many books on professional marketing, for example:

Gary Armstrong, Philip Kotler, Michael Harker and Ross Brennan. *Marketing —
An Introduction*. Pearson Education Limited, London, 2009.
Gerry Johnson, Richard Whittington and Kevin Scholes. *Fundamentals of
Strategy*. Pearson Education Limited, London, 2012.
Malcolm McDonald and Hugh Wilson. *Marketing Plans — How To Prepare
Them, How To Use Them*. John Wiley & Sons, Hoboken, 2011.
Richard A. Collier. *Profitable Product Management*. Butterworth-Heinemann,
Oxford, 1995.
Richard Koch. *The Financial Times Guide to Strategy*. Pearson Professional
Limited, London, 1995.

For guidance on research in the public interest, programme management
techniques are very useful:

Managing Successful Programmes. The Stationery Office, Crown Copyright
2007.

There are also many books on effective communication which can be useful when bidding for research contracts or writing brochures:

Caroline van den Brul. *Crackle and Fizz — Essential Communication and
Pitching Skills for Scientists*. Imperial College Press/World Scientific
Publishing Co. Pte Ltd., Singapore, 2014.

Daniel Kahneman. *Thinking, Fast and Slow*. Penguin Books, London, 2011.

Mark Forsyth. *The Elements of Eloquence — How to Turn the Perfect English Phrase*. Icon Books Ltd., London, 2013.

Sam Leith. *You Talkin' To Me? — Rhetoric from Aristotle to Obama*. Profile Books Ltd., London, 2011.

Steve Martin, Noah Goldstein and Robert B. Cialdini. *The Small BIG: Small Changes that Sparks Big Influence*. Profile Books Ltd., London, 2014.

Index

Printed in the United States
By Bookmasters